MY LOVE STORY

TINA TURNER

with Deborah Davis and Dominik Wichmann

ATRIA PAPERBACK

NEW YORK • LONDON • TORONTO • SYDNEY • NEW DELHI

ATRIA
PAPERBACK

An Imprint of Simon & Schuster, Inc.
1230 Avenue of the Americas
New York, NY 10020

Copyright © 2018 by Tina Turner

All rights reserved, including the right to reproduce this book or portions thereof in any form whatsoever. For information, address Atria Books Subsidiary Rights Department, 1230 Avenue of the Americas, New York, NY 10020.

First Atria Paperback edition September 2019

ATRIA PAPERBACK and colophon are trademarks of Simon & Schuster, Inc.

For information about special discounts for bulk purchases, please contact Simon & Schuster Special Sales at 1-866-506-1949 or business@simonandschuster.com.

The Simon & Schuster Speakers Bureau can bring authors to your live event. For more information or to book an event, contact the Simon & Schuster Speakers Bureau at 1-866-248-3049, or visit our website at www.simonspeakers.com.

Interior design by Dana Sloan

Manufactured in the United States of America

5 7 9 10 8 6

Library of Congress Cataloging-in-Publication Data has been applied for.

ISBN 978-1-5011-9824-3
ISBN 978-1-5011-9825-0 (pbk)
ISBN 978-1-5011-9826-7 (ebook)

"THERE'S ALWAYS BEEN AN EMOTION IN MY VOICE

BECAUSE IT REACHED BACK TO THE LIFE I WAS LIVING.

WHEN THERE WERE TEARS ONSTAGE, IT WASN'T

HOLLYWOOD, IT WAS REAL."

MY LOVE STORY

BETWEEN YOU AND ME

When I was a little girl, I loved taking chances. I'd swing over a creek in the backwoods of Nutbush, Tennessee, the place where I grew up, never thinking for a second what might happen if I fell into that swampy water. I tussled with animals—horses, mules, even snakes. I'm afraid of them now, but I wasn't when I was a child. I wasn't afraid of anything. One day, when I was playing in the woods, I found a little green snake and I thought, *Where did that one come from?* I was sure the baby had gotten separated from its mother. So I picked it up with a stick and went looking for the nest. Sure enough, when I found it, there was a big, ugly snake, ready to strike to protect its young. Immediately, instinct took over, not fear but self-preservation. I jumped up and ran as fast as I could, my braids coming undone and the sash of my dress falling off, until I was somewhere safe. The point is, *I knew when to run away from snakes.*

Throughout my life, there have been lots of times you might have asked me, "How did you get out of *that* one?" I did dangerous things, and dangerous things were done to me, but in the eleventh hour, something always told me when to run, how to survive. No matter what happened to me, I came through it every time. I decided, well, maybe I'm supposed to *live.* Maybe I'm here for a reason. And maybe the reason is to share my story with you.

You might be thinking, "Tina, we *know* your story. We know all about you and Ike, and the hell you lived through with him. We know you escaped from that terrible relationship, and that you endured." But, here's something that might surprise you. At this point in my life, I've spent far more time *without* Ike than with him. Forty-two years, to be exact. That's a whole second life, one with adventures, accomplishments, and love beyond my wildest dreams. But there's also been a dark side. During the past few years, I've faced life-and-death challenges I never, ever, expected. Let me tell you my story.

1

"THE BEST"

" Give me a lifetime of promises and a world of dreams

Speak the language of love like you know what it means **"**

"Tina, will you marry with me?" This was my first proposal from Erwin Bach, the love-at-first-sight love of my life, the man who made me feel dizzy the first time I saw him. His phrasing was a bit quaint—he's German, so English is not his first language—but I liked it. He was probably a little surprised when I said, "I don't have an answer." All I knew was that it wasn't yes and it wasn't no. This was in 1989, after we had been together for three years. I was turning fifty, and Erwin, who was thirty-three, thought I needed a commitment from him. He was gracious to offer, but I loved our relationship just the way it was. Plus, I wasn't certain how I felt about marriage. Marriage can change things and, in my experience, not always for the better.

Twenty-three years later (so much for not having a commitment), Erwin proposed again. This time, his timing was perfect. We were with a dozen close friends, cruising the Mediterranean on our friend Sergio's yacht, the *Lady Marina*. Looking back, I should have known something significant was about to happen. We were somewhere very pretty, but it wasn't romantic enough for Erwin. I found out later that he consulted Sergio, who suggested we sail to the Greek island of Skorpios. "Erwin, this is the best place I know for a most romantic moment," Sergio promised him.

That night, as the yacht changed direction and began speeding through the water to a new destination, I asked, "Where are we going, darling?" Erwin was vague and pretended not to know, which should have been a dead giveaway because Erwin *always* knows everything. The following morning, I awakened to the sight of beautiful Skorpios, the former Onassis retreat, with Jackie's famous blue-doored bathhouse silhouetted on the shore.

We spent a lazy day on the boat—I always found a shady spot to protect my skin while everyone else was basking in the sun—then separated to get ready for dinner. When we gathered with our friends for cocktails, all the men were wearing white. "That's nice," I thought. "They look really handsome in their white jeans and white shirts." And the ladies were equally well turned out in their summer finery. I was wearing a black linen dress, cool and elegant. We were having a wonderful time—great company, soft breezes, a moonlit evening. Then, after dinner, the atmosphere changed: suddenly, I could feel there was a sense of anticipation, even excitement, in the air. What was going on? I wondered.

I noticed that everyone had their eyes on Erwin, who walked up to me and knelt down on one knee. He was holding a small box in his outstretched hand—a timeless gesture. "I asked you before. Now I'll ask you again. Tina, will you marry me?" He said it in perfect English this time. The men were wiping their eyes—I couldn't get over that they were crying—and the women yelled "Whooohoo" as I answered him with an emphatic "Yes!" In that moment, I was saying yes to Erwin, and yes to love, a commitment that didn't come easily to me. I mean, here I was at the age of seventy-three and I was about to be a bride for the first time. That's right, for the *first* time. My name is Tina Turner, and I was married to Ike Turner, but I never was a bride.

Let me tell you about my wedding to Ike, if I can even call it a wedding. I wasn't the kind of girl who fantasized about growing up and having a big wedding. Sure, I imagined I would get married someday, but we didn't know about fancy weddings back in Nutbush—at least, not the kind where the bride wore white and a veil and all the trimmings. I don't remember any ceremonies like that because my parents and all my aunts and uncles had already gotten married by the time I came along (or they never married).

When Ike proposed to me, there was nothing romantic about it at all. He was trying to negotiate his way out of a tricky situation with one of his former wives who'd heard that we had a successful record and wanted to extract some money from him. Ike had been married so many times, I lost track—and all those wives were in addition to the countless girlfriends who came and went with dizzying speed. Ike slept with—or tried to sleep with—every woman in our orbit, married, single, and everything in between. I don't remember why marrying me was the solution to this particular financial problem, but in Ike's mind it was the right maneuver. Out of the blue, he said, "You want to marry me?" Just like that—gruff, terse, no niceties. That was Ike's way.

I didn't want to do it, and looking back, I now know how much I *really* didn't want to do it. By this time, I had seen and experienced Ike at his worst. But our lives were so complicated—together, we had a family of four children to raise (Ronnie, the son we had together; Craig, my son from a previous relationship; and Ike Jr. and Michael, the boys Ike had with his most recent wife, Lorraine), and we shared a career—so I didn't have much choice.

I figured if we were going to get married, I should at least look the part. I put on my best dress and a stylish brown hat with a wide brim.

Why a hat? I just felt it was the proper thing to do. I didn't want to look sexy, the way I did onstage or at a club, and I thought a hat would make me seem more serious and wedding-like. I tell you, when it came to social matters (and manners) there was no one around to guide me. I had to rely on my own instincts. I didn't have any friends because of Ike, so wherever we went, I was always watching people—in airports, in new cities, especially when we performed in Europe—watching and learning. I also read fashion magazines like *Vogue*, *Bazaar*, and *Women's Wear Daily*, constantly working to improve myself. That's where I learned how to dress, how to wear makeup, and how to develop a personal sense of style.

On the wedding day that didn't feel like a wedding day, I finished getting dressed and got into the backseat of the car with Ike. Duke, who was normally our bus driver, sat behind the wheel, ready to drive us over the border to Mexico. Duke and his wife, Birdie, who took care of our boys when we were on the road, were part of my extended family, so it was nice to have him along for the ride.

Ike always had an angle. He must have figured out that Tijuana was the best place for a quickie ceremony, that he could find someone to do it without a license or a blood test. It probably wasn't even legal. But there was no point in questioning his motives. It would just make him mad, and that might lead to a beating. I definitely didn't want a black eye on my wedding day.

Tijuana was seedy and honky-tonk in those days. Once we crossed over the border, we drove down a dusty road—God was it dusty— and found the Mexican version of a justice of the peace. In a small, dirty office, a man pushed some papers across a desk for me to sign, and that was it. I may not have had much experience with weddings, but I knew the occasion was supposed to be emotional and happy. There was none of that at this wedding. Nobody said, "You may kiss the bride." No toasts. No congratulations. No mention of living "happily ever after."

As bad as that was, what came next was even worse. As long as Ike was in down-and-dirty Tijuana, he wanted to have fun, *his* kind of fun. Guess where we went? To a whorehouse. On my wedding night! I've never, ever, told anyone this story because I was too embarrassed.

People can't imagine the kind of man he was—a man who takes his brand-new wife to a live, pornographic sex show right after their marriage ceremony. There I sat, in this filthy place, watching Ike out of the corner of my eye, wondering, *Does he really like this? How could he?* It was all so ugly. The male performer was unattractive and seemingly impotent, and the girl . . . well, let's just say that what was on display was more gynecological than erotic. I was miserable the whole time, on the verge of tears, but there was no escape. We couldn't leave until Ike was ready, and he was having a fine time.

The experience was so disturbing that I suppressed it—just scratched it out. By the time we drove back to Los Angeles, I had created a completely different scenario—a fantasy of a romantic elopement. By the next day, I was bragging to people, "Guess what? Oh, Ike took me to Tijuana. We got married yesterday!" I convinced myself that I was happy, and I *was* happy for a brief time, because the idea that I was married actually held meaning for me. For Ike, it was just another transaction: nothing had changed.

Well, if that wedding was a nightmare, the day I became Mrs. Erwin Bach was going to be a dream. No, a fairy tale, complete with a princess, a prince, and a castle! *Our* castle—the Château Algonquin, outside of Zurich, in Switzerland, where we had lived for fifteen years. This time, I decided to organize every detail myself. No wedding planner would be able to figure out what was in my head. I may have been crazy to take on all that responsibility, but I was determined to bring my fantasy to life, my way.

I like to get things done. First, I called my friend Jeff Leatham, the renowned floral designer I'd worked with for years, and asked him to transform the grounds of the château into a bower.

The all-important wedding dress was already hanging in my closet. I decided I didn't want to wear white, because the day wasn't all about me. Brides in big white wedding dresses get all the attention, and no one notices the groom. I didn't want to overpower Erwin. This was a marriage of two people. I have been wearing Giorgio Armani for decades, and I spotted this gorgeous gown, an irresistible confection of green taffeta, black silk tulle, and Swarovski crystals, at one of his runway shows in Beijing. When I tried it on, I had a real Cinderella moment. In fact, I loved it so much that I had to have it, "even if I never wear it," I told myself. But I knew in my heart that the gown was destined to be my wedding dress. Like most women, I don't have a perfect body—short neck and torso, prominent bosom, shall we say "mature" upper arms—but by the time the magicians at Armani finished their alterations, the dress was perfect. I added sheer black leggings and a wispy afterthought of a black veil, and Erwin pronounced it (and me) a work of art.

Does a bride have to have bridesmaids? I wondered. This was another instance where I was happy to break with tradition. Even though I have several close girlfriends, I didn't want to be surrounded by women on my wedding day. Somehow, that very thought took me back to the past, back to Ike and all the women he always kept around, the girlfriends and the one-night stands. Then I had a flash of inspiration. Our friends' children would be as fresh and as beautiful as Jeff Leatham's flowers, so why not have them as our wedding party? I invited four adorable little girls and one darling boy to join us on the big day, and I arranged for them to meet me at Giorgio Armani. I wanted my little flower girls to have gowns as fanciful as mine, but in a different color. Armani designed a dress fit for a young princess, in a beautiful shade of lilac pink.

Erwin asked his brother, Jürgen Bach, to be his best man and, for my maid of honor, I turned to one of the constants in my life, Rhonda Graam. When I first met Rhonda in 1964, she was a young "Ike and Tina" fan—a California girl who was into music. She'd stayed close to me in so many roles—friend, confidante, assistant, road manager—for almost fifty years, and we'd supported each other through all kinds of situations. Rhonda was my connection to the past, while the children represented the future. Something old, something new, I thought.

Erwin and I carefully put together a guest list, inviting family and our closest friends. Ever practical, he warned that with celebrities in attendance like Oprah and my old friend singer Bryan Adams, we would have to arrange for security because the wedding would attract a lot of attention. That meant I'd have to sacrifice my beloved view of Lake Zurich for the day because we had to put up a tall red screen to block our property from the water. If we could see out, then the paparazzi could see in, and we wanted privacy.

Jeff Leatham outdid himself. More than a hundred thousand roses in shades of red, pink, orange, yellow, and white came from Holland in freezer trucks. I'd never seen such beautiful flowers in my whole life, and the air was filled with the most wonderful scent. It took days to create the arrangements. Jeff had people working all over the grounds, even in the trees. Madness everywhere. There was no living in the house with all that going on. So Erwin and I moved into a suite at the Dolder Grand Hotel in Zurich, and I came back every day to check on the progress. It got to the point when I got so tired of even *thinking* about the wedding that I fantasized about hopping into the car and running away to Italy for an early honeymoon.

I think all brides and grooms have fights and disagreements before their wedding. Erwin and I argued about the weather. "*Schatzi*," he'd say to me, using the German word for sweetheart, "what if it rains? We have to have a Plan B." I had no interest in being practical. "No," I said, "no Plan B. The garden is too beautiful. I'm not covering it up with a tent." We had consulted the *Farmers' Almanac* and picked a day that seemed to be good with the stars, the moon, and the universe. But, that wasn't good enough for Erwin. During the setup, I walked into the garden and saw that someone had smuggled in tent poles to keep in reserve in case it rained. "Take them away," I insisted. "I don't want a tent. It's *not* going to rain!"

Next hurdle: as I sat admiring the flowers and the tables—twenty antique glass columns set with china and my own collection of crystal—workers walked by with large umbrellas and began assembling them. They were positioning them to block drones, they explained. Drones? At my wedding? That's definitely a twenty-first-century problem! I stood up and announced, "I'm not attending this wedding anymore. I'm leaving now." I walked away and stayed away until the unsightly umbrellas came down. I wasn't going to let anyone ruin my decorations. Not even drones.

———

Just as I predicted, there was no rain on July 21, 2013. But the weather had a wicked sense of humor and played a big joke on us because it turned out to be the hottest day of the year—a record-breaking scorcher. We laid out individual paper fans for our guests in case the heat became too oppressive. I've always thought that having a proper fan is a bit nicer than waving a menu, or whatever else is at hand, to create a breeze.

Erwin and I had planned on getting ready at the hotel, but at the last minute, we decided to pack up our wedding clothes and dress at our home. I'm so glad we did because it was more festive to be with the other members of the wedding party—especially the children. I helped them put the finishing touches on their hair and dresses—I was really hands-on—and gave each one a special little Cartier bracelet to commemorate the occasion. Then we sent them off to the nearby guesthouse to wait for the wedding procession to begin. The "coach" that would carry our little prince and princesses the short distance to their ceremonial entrance was a very unusual white Rolls-Royce. The front of the car was classic, but the back had been converted into a pickup truck where the children could all sit. We covered the car with garlands of flowers.

At some point, it dawned on me that I wouldn't be able to see anything until the ceremony began. I told Erwin, "You know what, darling? I feel sad that I'm going to miss the first part of the wedding and only get to see it in the photographs afterwards." We thought about it and figured out a solution so I didn't have to miss a thing. I've been a Buddhist for over forty years, and I have a beautiful prayer room on the second floor of the house, where I go every day to chant and pray at my *butsudan*. It is glassed in and overlooks the front of the house. I set myself up in that perfect spot, sat quietly, and watched. Most people think of me as being in perpetual motion: dancing across a stage; strutting down a staircase; even hanging from the Eiffel Tower. But life has taught me that some of my most meaningful and memorable moments happen when I'm in repose, sitting, meditating, contemplating. Peering through my window, watching our guests arrive, gave me the opportunity to realize just how important they were to me, and how happy I was that they were with us on our special day.

On a more frivolous note, I also got to see how fabulous they looked! Our invitation specified a dress code—white for the women and black tie for the men. I acknowledge that it *is* unusual to ask women to wear white to a wedding, but I had my reasons. The designer in me didn't want random colors competing with our carefully composed décor. I also knew that people would look glamorous in classic black and white . . . and they did! White looked beautiful against the greenery and the flowers; it was so picturesque. Later, several of the ladies said to me something along the lines of "Tina, my dress was hard to find, but you were right."

I enjoyed seeing the guests' reactions as they stepped into the magical setting we had created for them: the front of the house was draped with oversized floral boas, the grounds a fantasy come to life. I wanted a Garden of Eden effect, with cascades of blossoms and banks of greenery everywhere, and it turned out just as I had imagined. Jeff Leatham even constructed an enormous hedge of 140,000 bright red roses, which I saw as a nod to my trademark red lips. I took one look at it and said, "That's me!"

I am Rock 'n' Roll—*Tina Turner* is Rock 'n' Roll—and I can't envision performing any other way. But there is another side of me, the

Tina who wears ballet flats and pearls, who believes in elegance: on my wedding day, I wanted my garden, my house, my guests—myself—to be the best that we could be. When I saw my friends strolling through the grounds, sipping champagne, I felt like I was watching a scene from *The Great Gatsby*.

Eventually, I had to pull myself away from the view to put on my dress. At the appointed hour, the children, precious cargo, arrived in their festive vehicle. Their beaming fathers helped them out and lined them up for the wedding march. It was the prettiest sight—they were so excited. The older girls swanned down the aisle, practically dancing. The youngest, an angel with long blond curls, barely knew how to scatter the rose petals from her basket. Our handsome page boy was sweet and shy. He was so serious that he made everyone smile. Those children stole the hearts of all the guests.

Erwin, who is a car enthusiast and knows everything about them, selected my black Rolls-Royce convertible for our entrance. He was at the wheel, as usual, while I sat by his side, not at all nervous, just happy. As you might expect, we put a lot of thought into our choice of wedding music. If you listen to Frank Sinatra's "My Way," the words fit my life perfectly. *"The record shows I took the blows | And did it my way."* I had to have that one! The song built to its dramatic climax as we arrived, and it was a very emotional moment for us and our loved ones.

We walked down the aisle to the music of our friend Bryan Adams, who played his guitar and serenaded us with his romantic ballad "All for Love." The song has the beauty and power of a vow set to music. A wedding vow. *"Let's make it all for one and all for love,"* Bryan sang, and I ended up singing a few lines with him. How could I resist?

———

The ceremony was traditional, with a few "Tina touches." The backdrop behind the officiant was a wall of white, yellow, orange, and pink roses arranged in a beautiful tree-of-life design, which is a symbol of knowledge, creativity, and immortality. Dear friends said a few words about our history together. A few weeks earlier, on July 4, Erwin and I had exchanged rose-gold wedding bands (engraved with the letters "T" and "E") at a civil ceremony in Zurich, so technically we were already married. But it felt different to be surrounded by a loving and enthusiastic group of witnesses who never stopped smiling. They were so happy and excited. They looked at us as if we were the center of the universe, and I liked that! With the words "You may kiss and embrace each other with God's blessing," we were a couple in every way, a couple with a *commitment*.

After the ceremony, during a chorus of congratulations, we gathered on the stairs for photographs. That's when I started to feel a little funny. *It must be the heat*, I thought, or the dress, which was getting heavier by the minute. I tried to ignore my discomfort until it got the better of me, and I let Rhonda lead me inside the house. I sat in the dining room for about half an hour, trying to compose myself, praying the sensation would pass. I didn't want to miss a minute of the wedding, and here I was in a chair, wondering when I would feel well enough to join my own party. Eventually, sheer willpower propelled me to my feet and I walked outside. I didn't want to think about it, so I just pushed the troubling episode out of my mind and focused on enjoying my wedding.

I like food that's spicy and exotic, so that's what we served—thinly sliced beef with coriander and vegetables, Tom Yum Goong, which is a Thai hot-and-sour soup, and a banquet of other tasty and beautifully plated dishes. At one point, I heard Oprah say, "Ummm . . . I don't know what it is, but it's *really* good!" The children had their own little fairy table under a tree. Instead of a traditional cake, we had a gorgeous, five-foot tower of miniature tarts—fruit, cream, marzipan—a dream come true for me and anyone else with a sweet tooth.

I had worked for months to organize the wedding, and fretted over every last detail, yet there were two wonderful surprises in store for me. During dinner, we were told to look up at the sky. A helicopter flew over the house, and suddenly it was raining rose petals! Friends had arranged this for us, and it was such a romantic thing to have happen.

Erwin came up with the real high point of the evening. I don't know how he did it, because he is generally a little quiet and reserved. He and about fifteen of his friends walked out in front of the crowd and sat down with sombreros pulled down on their heads—like hombres. The music started and boom! All the guys jumped up and started dancing with their guitars. They weren't really playing, of course, but the lively gypsy music and their energetic steps roused all our guests from their seats. The whole place lit up. I have to hand it to Erwin: I'm the entertainer, but *he* stole the show. It was *the* moment, the one people still talk about when they remember Tina and Erwin's wedding.

After everyone left, I walked down to the lake alone and sat down at one of the tables. I was exhausted, my beautiful dress was squeezing me, and I welcomed the chance to take off my shoes, rest, and enjoy the quiet. I looked back at the decorated house, beautiful, just the way I wanted it. Then I looked up. God had given us a clear, clear sky and the most glorious moon, which bathed the garden in an incredible light. As I looked at that moon, it seemed to be looking right back at me, blessing our union. It was magical. I'd known it wouldn't rain on my wedding because, when you've suffered as long as I have, you deserve some kind of reward. Every single thing I'd done, every choice I'd made—on my wedding day, and in my life for that matter—was from instinct, and it ended up being exactly right.

I'd labored all my life. Nobody gave me one thing. After so many years of hard work and, frankly, hard times, I looked forward to living in the moment with Erwin, to rising peacefully each day without worry, want, or agenda. *I've reached my nirvana,* I thought. That complete happiness when you wish for nothing. It's a wonderful place to be.

———

Three months later, I woke up suddenly and in a panic. A lightning bolt struck my head and my right leg—at least that's how it felt—and I had a funny sensation in my mouth that made it difficult for me to call out to Erwin for help. I suspected it wasn't good, but it was worse than I ever imagined.

I was having a stroke.

———

2

"BACK WHERE YOU STARTED"

> " Who's going to
> help ya, throw
> you a lifeline? "

I 'm sitting in a dialysis chair at a hospital in Zollikon, Switzerland, only ten minutes from my home, trying to ignore death tapping me on the shoulder, saying, "Tina . . . Tina, I'm here." I'm desperately trying to stay healthy, or as close to healthy as someone with 5 percent kidney function can get, while I wait impatiently for my body to be strong enough to accept my only possible salvation—a potentially life-saving kidney transplant.

"Wait," you might say, "I'm confused. Weren't you having a stroke?"

Darling, I'm confused, too. I've been on such a wild roller-coaster ride during the four years since my wedding that even *I* have difficulty keeping my medical catastrophes straight. High blood pressure. Stroke. Intestinal cancer. No! No! Wrong order. Stroke. Vertigo, or *Der Schwindel*, as they call it in Switzerland, *then* intestinal cancer. And now, kidney failure. I need more than the proverbial nine lives to survive everything that's been thrown at me.

I have to report to the clinic several times a week. Thanks to Erwin, who is very careful and protective, our routine is always the same. On treatment days, he parks in front of the Château Algonquin at exactly the same time, and in such a way that I can go straight from the steps to the car. He's such a gentleman that he's already opened the passenger door. Then, we drive to a small bakery in Küsnacht, not far from the train station. I stay in the car so that no one recognizes me, while Erwin runs in to buy an assortment of Swiss pastry. This way, we'll have something nice to eat during the long hours ahead.

The trip to the clinic is always a tense game of hide-and-seek. Somehow, we've managed to keep the fact that I'm seriously ill an absolute secret for several years. This is possible because we live in Switzerland, where people have considerably more respect for privacy than in other countries. And Erwin and I have developed a precise system to ensure that no one recognizes us, especially in the clinic, where I would be easy prey for paparazzi.

When we arrive, Erwin parks at a back entrance. From there it's a short walk directly into the dialysis rooms. I usually wear a black cape in the winter, or a heavy coat with a large hat, so that I can hide behind all of that fabric. Erwin and I are silent on the way in so no one can hear my voice and figure out that I'm speaking English. Otherwise, passersby might recognize me and take a photo to sell to the media.

I'm not assigned a private room—I would be upset if the staff gave me one because I've never been a diva. I want to be treated like everyone else, not stand out just because I've had a little more luck in my life. The doctors make some allowances because, like me, they want to avoid photographers. Whenever possible, my appointments are scheduled at quiet times, when there isn't very much patient activity, and the nurses close off my area with a curtain.

I try to make my time in the chair as pleasant as possible. I eat the pastry, when I can stomach it, and read my books. Weirdly, I tend to bring the same three books each time: *The Book of Secrets* by Deepak Chopra, *The Divine Comedy* by Dante, and a book of photography by the extraordinary Horst P. Horst. Something for the spirit, something for the intellect, and something for the senses. I never get tired of these books, which stimulate deep thoughts and feelings within me. I turn to them repeatedly for inspiration and comfort.

Day in, day out, I maintain these rituals while my blood is being washed. Read, fall asleep, wake up, drift. I think about Erwin. I replay memories of my late mother and sister, my children, my own childhood. And I'm surprised to find myself thinking about Ike. I keep saying that I'm finished with all that, but here he is again, calling for my attention. I reexamine the early days, the bad times, my decision to leave him and start a new life. Many of these thoughts have been on my mind before, but never so vividly. This time, I'm asking myself questions and looking for answers. You think differently about your life when faced with your own death.

How did I get from a fantasy wedding at a château on Lake Zurich to a dialysis chair? That's a long story. How did I get from Nutbush, Tennessee, to that château? That's an even *longer* one. When I'm tethered to the dialysis machine, I see everything through the piercing lens of mortality. I have all the time in the world. Time to think about the past, what it means to me in the present, and the *big* question: will I have a future?

I believe that in order for you to really know my story, you have to know where—and what—I came from. My struggle began at birth, on November 26, 1939, when I entered the world as Anna Mae Bullock. Ever since then, I have spent my entire life fighting my way through a climate of bad karma. What did it feel like to be an unwanted child? What was that child's life like? How did that child prevail in spite of the many strikes against her?

Let me tell you all about that.

There was a shadow looming over my earliest years, and it was cast

---

by someone who was absent more than she was present: my mother, Zelma Currie Bullock, whom we called "Muh," the first syllable of the word "mother." She was a spoiled little girl who grew up to be a spoiled adult. Her daddy favored her over her three brothers, encouraging her to think that she could reach out and take whatever she wanted in life. When she grew up, that included my father, Floyd Richard Bullock. She stole him from another girl, just because she could. That's how they got together, which never should have happened in the first place. Their marriage was a battlefield from the beginning, right through the birth of their first child, my sister Alline. Then, when Muh finally decided they should separate once and for all, she found out she was pregnant with me and had no choice but to stay.

My mother was a woman who bore children, but she never really wanted them, especially not a rambunctious baby like me. I was totally different from Alline. I was the tomboy, always in motion, doing everything I could to force Muh to pay attention to me. Even as a child, when I watched how she treated my sister, I knew there was a difference. She'd look at Alline's face and caress her affectionately, and I'd think, *That's nice*, because I loved my sister. But I wished she'd do the same to me. Muh had a gentle touch when she combed Alline's hair, which was soft and fine. When it was my turn, she impatiently tugged and pulled at my head because my unruly hair was woolly, not pretty like Alline's, and much harder to comb. Maybe she found it harder because it was mine.

She didn't punish Alline with the switch as much as she whipped me, because my sister was better behaved. In Muh's eyes, I was too active. I was either in trouble, or *was* trouble, so I always seemed to be running away from her and her switch—hiding under the bed, climbing a tree, anything to escape the *whoosh* of that stick, with its hard, little point that stung and made a popping sound when it hit the skin.

I knew then that my mother didn't love me. I wonder now if she loved anyone other than herself and maybe Alline. She didn't love my father. My earliest memory of my parents was of them fighting. Although, for better or for worse, Muh could hold her own in any argument. She was a strong, fearless woman who knew how to take care of herself. She used to sit at the window on a stool, thinking her way out. When she'd had enough, *she* was the one who walked out the door, not caring who, or what, she left behind.

I was eleven years old when my mother abandoned us. It was 1950, and Alline and I had been in that sorry position before, when our parents moved five hours away from Nutbush to find better paying jobs in Knoxville during World War II. But they often sent for us to visit them, and eventually they came back. This time was different. I was at a tender and complicated age. School was difficult. *Life* was difficult. Oh, how I needed a mother! I ran through the house in a panic looking for her. I went to the mailbox, wishing for a letter that would give me some connection to Muh. But, of course, she couldn't write because my father would figure out where she was. When he did find out where she was living in St. Louis, he sent me and Alline to visit her, hoping the sight of her daughters would make her want to come home.

"Come here, baby," she cooed when she saw me. What right did she have to call me *baby*? I wondered. Whenever Muh tried to be nice, I didn't believe her. I couldn't believe her. It was safer to keep my distance. She never came back and I avoided visiting her.

Looking back on our relationship now, I realize Muh and I were either estranged or at odds with each other our whole lives. But that

---

didn't prevent me from being a good daughter and taking care of her after I became successful and had the money to do so. I made sure she had a nice house and nice things, no matter how much friction there was between us. When I was living in London in the late 1980s, I went to a psychic who told me, "You weren't wanted when you were born and you even knew it when you were inside your mother." She confirmed what I had always felt when I was growing up.

When I told Muh what the psychic said, she started to cry. Trying to defend herself (although there was no defense), she said, "I saved your life." She meant that on one occasion when she was fighting with my father, she did something to protect me from getting hurt. I didn't let her get away with *that*. I said, "I'll bet you're happy you did, Muh, because look where you are now!" More than anything, Muh loved the status that came with being Tina Turner's mother. I wanted her to know that by "saving" me, she had really saved herself.

I guess you could say I was born with a Buddha nature inside of me, because the miracle is that I didn't give up. With all the instability and pain in my life, especially my troubled relationship with my mother, I was still a happy, carefree, and optimistic child, and I've kept that attitude my whole life. People ask me, "Where do you get such strength?" I tell them I was born with it. I've always been strong and independent. I had struggles, but I was also given the strength to endure them. I've always been able to find the good in any situation.

I enjoyed growing up in Nutbush, a don't-blink-or-you'll-miss-it little town on Highway 19 in Tennessee, and I wouldn't change a thing, except I hated working in the cotton fields. No, thank you, I could live without that. We were comfortable in our shotgun house, one story with all the rooms situated one behind the other, as is the style in the

South (the old saying was that you could shoot a gun from the front door straight through to the back). We weren't poor like some. Our garden was big and plentiful, so we ate well. We were a part of a lively community of family and friends. Everyone worked hard, played hard, and worshipped at church on Sunday.

I had two grandmothers, my father's mother, Mama Roxanna Bullock, who was very strict, and my mother's mother, Mama Georgie Currie, who was kind and fun-loving. There was no question that I preferred spending time with Mama Georgie. The atmosphere at her house was happy and lively, while life at Mama Roxanna's was harsh and all about rules.

I loved being a country girl, and that's how I learned to be independent. My father was the overseer at a farm and my parents left me at home while they went to work in the fields. I was young—small enough to need a chair to get my glass of milk and a snack—but old enough to entertain myself, although not always in the best way. If there was a tree, I climbed it, never giving a thought to falling down. If there was excitement, or danger, I found it. I took chances, and I remember staring death in the face a few times.

It seemed that on every farm, there was a horse that didn't like children. We were told to stay away, but one day, I was tired of playing alone and wanted to run across the way to my grandmother's place. I thought maybe I could sneak past that nasty horse. I opened the door quietly—but you know those animals have another sense. He heard my little steps and came charging after me.

Mama Georgie's house wasn't far, but for a little girl running from an angry animal, it seemed like a mile. I managed to reach the fence, yelling because the horse had gotten to me and was about to pull me down and trample me. Suddenly, one of our billy goats ran over to distract the horse, bleating his little heart out like a Disney character. When the horse looked away, my cousin Margaret rushed in at the last minute to pull me to safety. I don't know what my father did with the horse, but that goat was my hero. I always believed that he saved my life.

Danger aside, I was happiest when I was outdoors. Children adapt when life is hard. They find something to help them get through it. I was always out of the house, exploring, playing in the neighboring pastures, fields, and gardens, watching animals, looking at the sky. Home, especially when my mother was there, could be unpleasant. After she left, it was just sad. But nature was my special retreat, a world of love and harmony to me. Even when I went there hurt and angry, it would transform me. "Where have you been all day?" I was asked when I came home, dreamy and disheveled. Where *had* I been? Nowhere in particular, just being outside made me feel good.

I did not feel the same way about going to school. Like other rural schools at the time, the Flagg Grove School in Nutbush was one big room, made of clapboard, and shared by three classes that were taught simultaneously. I was not a good student, so I lived in fear of being called to the blackboard. One day, my teacher asked me to come up to solve an arithmetic problem. Panic set in. I freaked out because I had no idea how to do it. I remember falling to the floor, kicking and crying because all eyes were on me, and everyone in the room could see that I didn't know the answer.

Looking back, I think the teacher should have intervened, but in those days, I don't even know if they were aware of children who had learning disabilities, and I was definitely one of those children. I felt totally alone, helpless, embarrassed. Not that I would have said the word "embarrassed" then: I would have said "ashamed"—ashamed that I was standing there in front of all the other kids, failing, with numbers blurring in front of me because of my tears. My brain didn't have that ability. I called it "not smart," and I suffered because I believed I had to hide my stupidity from my family and friends and, when I got older, my coworkers and managers.

My attitude changed later in life, in more informed times, when my doctors told me there was a reason why I had difficulty learning. It had something to do with my frontal lobes. The creative part of my brain was ablaze and working overtime, but I would never be good at counting or reading. I finally got over my lifelong sense of inadequacy when Princess Beatrice, Queen Elizabeth's granddaughter, discussed her dyslexia in a number of interviews. I know that other people have spoken about this condition, but there was something about the way she explained it that made me pay attention. She said that she wasn't able to count and that she had a hard time learning how to read. She could have been describing me. For the first time, I truly understood what my problem was, and felt better about myself.

There's a Buddhist expression, "turning poison into medicine." That's the best way to describe what happened to the Flagg Grove School, the scene of my many humiliations at the blackboard. The historian Henry Louis Gates researched my ancestry on his PBS program *African American Lives*, and discovered that my great-grandfather, Benjamin Flagg, was the original owner of the property that was the site for the school. He sold the land for less than market value so the school could be built and black children would have a place to go for an education. I was profoundly moved by that revelation.

Then, a few years ago, I was approached by the West Tennessee Delta Heritage Center. They proposed moving the old school from Nutbush to nearby Brownsville to turn it into the Tina Turner Museum. They wanted to celebrate my career in music and to show people what it was like to attend an African American school in the South in the 1940s. The school had been closed for years (it had become a barn) and needed a lot of work. We raised enough money to transport the building to a new site, where it was painstakingly restored and outfitted with Tina Turner memorabilia. The windows were made to appear as if they were looking out at a cotton field. The museum opened in 2014, with my costumes and gold records standing beside my original wooden schoolgirl desk and, of all things, an authentic chalkboard, just like the one that terrified me when I was a child. It doesn't scare me anymore. Now I'd like to think it inspires people to overcome whatever obstacles they may experience in life, turning *their* poison into medicine.

The Anna Mae who cried in front of the class was one side of me. The *other* Anna Mae was a born entertainer who, under the right circumstances, would have *welcomed* the attention and done anything to hold on to it. If at the very moment of my humiliation someone had said, "Wait! Start the music!" I immediately would have jumped up off the floor with a big smile on my face, singing, dancing, and performing like crazy. I was confident and never ashamed to do it—no stage fright whatsoever. Even as a little girl, I knew I could sing better than the grown women around me. I was *born* with that talent. My voice was my gift and I knew how to use it.

I have been singing my entire life. Some of my earliest memories are of my mother taking me shopping when she and my father lived in Knoxville. Unlike Nutbush, Knoxville was a big city with all kinds of stores. When the salesgirls found out that I could sing, they put me up on a stool—I was maybe four or five at the time—and listened while I performed my versions of the latest hits. "I was walking along, singing a song," I sang without hesitation. As soon as I heard a song on the radio, I instantly had it, memorized almost every word on the spot. It was natural and effortless, like a snake shedding one skin for another. I was born with that. The salesgirls thought that I, the little girl with the big voice, was so entertaining they gave me shiny coins, dimes, nickels, quarters, even fifty-cent pieces, a fortune in my eyes, that I kept in a glass bank. They were my first paying audience!

Knoxville was also the home of the "sanctified church," where we worshipped whenever we were in town. I didn't know what "sanctified" meant, but I loved that it was totally different from our Baptist church back in Nutbush. When the congregation got what they called the "Spirit," they danced, clapped their hands, and sang at the top of their lungs. They were possessed by God and music. I sang and danced right along with them. It felt like being in a show, especially when it got loud and fast. I didn't understand the particulars of their religion, but the spectacle—the sound, the movement, the pure joy—was really exciting.

Back in Nutbush, my family was my captive audience. At Mama Georgie's we—Alline, my half sister Evelyn (my mother had a child before she met my father), my cousins, and me performed shows we made up on the spot. I never had to think about singing or dancing for a second—what to do, or how to do it. I was the leader, always taking charge of the others, picking the songs and demonstrating the steps. We had so much fun pretending to be onstage. I had a photograph from that time, but when Alline grew up, she decided that she didn't like how she looked, so she destroyed it. That really made me suffer because it was the only picture I had of myself when I was skinny and all voice.

I loved singing at picnics. Everybody had picnics, but in Nutbush, black people's picnics were different, more fun I think, with fresh barbecue piled up on the tables and a real carnival atmosphere. For live entertainment, we had Mr. Bootsy Whitelaw, who was famous in our part of Tennessee. He played the trombone, while another musician accompanied him on the snare drum. A marching band wouldn't have been as exciting to me as those two. I soon became known far and wide as the "little Anna Mae" who sang with Mr. Bootsy. I don't remember what songs he played for me to sing, but I was right there by his side, loudly and enthusiastically trying to rouse the crowd to join in. "Come sing with Mr. Bootsy," I called to the passersby. Bootsy Whitelaw made such an impression on me that years later, when I was with Ike, I wrote and recorded a song about him (*"Bop along, bop along, bop along, Mr. Bootsy Whitelaw"*).

I never stood still for a moment when I was singing. I was always doing a little dance step, whether it was a choreographed step or whatever. My sister could not dance. My mother could not dance. But *I* could. I think when you can sing, the dancing goes with the singing.

Singing was both a form of expression and a source of comfort to me, especially when my living situation became unpredictable and I was shuttled from place to place. Muh was gone, and then, when I was thirteen, my father moved away and disappeared from our lives. Alline and I lived with some cousins for a time, then we settled in with Mama Roxanna, who watched our every move. I found security and affection with Connie and Guy Henderson, a young white couple who needed help with their baby. I loved living in their house and I considered myself a part of their family. I craved order and routine after going through so much upheaval in my life.

The Hendersons set a wonderful example for me because they had high standards. They taught me how to maintain a lovely home, which they filled with books, magazines, and pretty things. They gave me guidance about proper manners. They even took me on a trip to Dallas, Texas, so I saw a little bit of the world outside of Tennessee. More importantly, they showed me that a married couple could be loving to each other and live in harmony with their children. This kind of behavior may seem normal, but it wasn't my experience.

I wanted a relationship of my own, and when I was fifteen, I found it with Harry Taylor, the high school basketball player who was my first love. Harry was perfect in every way—handsome, popular, the captain of the team. I was so thrilled to be with him that I put up with his behavior—he would break up with me, see another girl, then come back—because I imagined we would settle down and get married someday. Of course, I had all the wisdom of a fifteen-year-old when I hatched this plan. Harry broke my heart when one of his other girlfriends became pregnant and he married her. I was in no hurry to experience that kind of disappointment again.

Hoping for a fresh start, I went to live with Mama Georgie. I believed I was old enough to make these decisions myself, although no one seemed to care enough to question my choices.

Just a few months later, when I was sixteen and still in high school,

Mama Georgie died. I felt so alone without her, and I had no idea what I would do. Then my mother invited me to live with her in St. Louis. Alline was already there. I was apprehensive about moving in with Muh after having been away from her for so long, but I was intrigued by the idea of living in a big city. I was no longer a vulnerable child who needed her mother. Now I knew how to protect myself, or at least I thought I did.

Experience had taught me that when I dared to care about someone, I lost them; Muh, when she moved away; my beloved cousin Margaret, who died in a car accident; Harry, who broke my young heart when he left me for another girl; Mama Georgie; and now I had to say goodbye to the Hendersons.

I never felt loved, so I decided it wasn't important. Not to me. I think I put up a kind of a shield against it. I told myself, "If you don't care about me, that's okay, I'll go on. If you don't love me, I'll go on." *I'll go on* was my mantra before I ever knew what a mantra was.

3

"SOMETHING'S GOT A HOLD ON ME"

> **"**I get a feeling, I feel so strange
>
> Everything about me seems to have changed**"**

I n St. Louis, I was feeling a little lost and lonely in my new life, so I was thrilled when Alline, who was sexy and sophisticated (and, unlike me, had an adult social life that involved lipstick, high heels, and men in Cadillacs), offered to take me to a nightclub in racy East St. Louis. The band that filled the place every night was Ike Turner and the Kings of Rhythm. Of course, I had heard of them, everybody had. Ike's "Rocket 88," one of the very first rock 'n' roll songs ever, was a big hit, although typical of the record business at the time, he didn't make any money on it. Ike Turner was the most popular and hardworking musician on the St. Louis/East St. Louis club circuit. He was always in the newspapers, and I was excited to have the chance to hear him play in person at the Club Manhattan.

The first time I saw Ike onstage he was at his very best, sharply dressed in a dark suit and tie. Ike wasn't conventionally handsome— actually, he wasn't handsome at all—and he certainly wasn't my type. Remember, I was a schoolgirl, all of seventeen, looking at a man. I was used to high school boys who were clean-cut, athletic, and dressed in denim, so Ike's processed hair, diamond ring, and skinny body—he was all edges and sharp cheekbones—looked old to me, even though he was only twenty-five. I'd never seen anyone that thin! I couldn't help thinking, *God, he's ugly.*

I was definitely in the minority. Most women, black or white, found Ike irresistible because there was something dangerous about him. And Ike didn't just *look* dangerous: he *was* dangerous. There were endless rumors about his bad temper, his flare-ups with his musicians, his fights with jealous women (and sometimes their angry husbands), and there was the story about that time he beat up someone with a gun, earning him the nickname "Pistol Whippin'" Ike Turner. *That* Ike Turner was an angry and unpredictable man with an infamous dark side, but at the time, there was a glamour to that.

Despite his reputation for being an outlaw, Ike had a personality that people liked. He was fun. Kind of Southern. He didn't speak proper English, but you knew it was his way. He really had something when he came out onstage and lit it up. He picked up his guitar, or sat at the piano, and brought the instrument to life. People just went crazy. Like me. That's who *I* responded to that first night, a great guitarist playing the most exciting music, music that made me want to burst into song and dance. Alline was dating one of the guys in the band, so she was always following them from one club to another. I begged her to let me tag along. With my sister as chaperone, I became a regular at the Club Manhattan and anywhere else they were playing.

The atmosphere between sets was so casual that sometimes Ike invited a girl in the audience to come up and sing at the microphone. I wanted to be that girl. A dozen times, I imagined how I'd jump up on the stage, hold the mike gracefully, as if I'd been doing it my whole life, and sing with a voice so powerful it would rock the room. But night after night, Ike passed me by, selecting girls who were prettier and sexier, but who couldn't sing a note. If he noticed me at all, and I doubt that he did, I was just "Little Ann," Alline's invisible younger sister.

One night, Alline's boyfriend tried to tease her into singing during the break. She turned him down flat, pushing the mike away. I saw my opportunity and grabbed it. Ike was onstage, playing B.B. King's "You Know I Love You." I started singing, my voice cutting through the noise and the smoke, forcing everyone, including Ike, to take another look at Little Ann. He was shocked when he heard my voice. It didn't sound like it could come from such a skinny young girl. He loved what he heard that night, and it was the *music*, not the usual boy/girl, man/woman thing, that drew us together.

Suddenly, I found myself in a world I'd never imagined. Think of me, a teenager and still a country girl at heart, naïve and eager as a puppy for affection and acceptance. Ike was older. He already had a woman, Lorraine (actually, he probably had twenty women, but that shows just how naïve I really was). Ike and I became fast friends, like brother and sister, not lovers. He was impressive, with his hot band, his pink Cadillac, his big house in East St. Louis. Even Muh, who didn't want me hanging around with the wrong people, had to admit Ike had a charm all his own.

The best part was that I got to sing professionally. Back in Tennessee, if you enjoyed singing, you had three options: singing along with the radio, singing at a church, or singing at a picnic with Mr. Bootsy Whitelaw. But this was the real thing, performing on a stage, with a popular band. Ike taught me all about music *and* he paid me to sing. When we weren't performing, we lived and breathed music, whether we were rehearsing or making late night rounds of the clubs. We had fun together—so much fun—and that was it.

When I wanted romance, I found it with Raymond Hill, a handsome young man who was more my type than Ike. He played saxophone with the Kings of Rhythm and lived in Ike's house with the other musicians who worked in the band. Romance led to sex, and in short order, I became pregnant. Muh was not pleased. Especially after Raymond broke his ankle and moved home to Clarksdale, Mississippi, to recover, and that was the last of him. I was all alone. In 1958, at the age of eighteen, I gave birth to a beautiful baby boy I named Raymond Craig. I was young, strong, and quick to recover, and I wanted to make a good life for my son.

When I wasn't singing, I was working as an aide at a hospital to support us, and I flirted with the idea of studying to be a nurse. Who was I kidding? I liked dressing up in the fancy clothes Ike bought me—long gloves, sparkly earrings, and pretty dresses—and enjoyed stepping out on the stage like a star. I wanted to *sing*. That meant more Ike, more time spent at his house, and then, the night when we crossed the line.

There was a party at Ike's house. I was staying over, and one of the guys made some comment about coming to my room later. There was no lock on my door so, to protect myself, I stayed with Ike. That wasn't unusual. I had spent innocent nights there before, like a sleepover. This time, we drifted into something sexual. It was inevitable with Ike. I think we were both surprised, uncomfortable, unsure of how to move forward. I was so young. What did I know? Since it was easier to keep going than to try to get back the friendship we'd had before, that's what we did. Then, in 1960, I discovered I was expecting Ike's child.

Sex was awkward for us, but that wasn't the real problem. Looking back, I realize that my relationship with Ike was doomed the day he figured out that I was going to be his meal ticket, his moneymaker. He was scheduled to record "A Fool in Love," a song he'd written for a male singer named Art Lassiter, until they had some sort of falling out. The studio was booked, so I was called in to replace Art on the vocals. I made the song my own. Ironically, "A Fool in Love" tells the story of woman who's fallen in love with a man who abuses her in some way. The lyrics, *"You know you love him, you can't understand | Why he treats you like he do when he's such a good man,"* ended up being prophetic. Juggy Murray, the head of Sue Records, heard my version, loved it, paid Ike $25,000 for the rights, and told him to make "that girl" the star of his act.

What went through Ike's head when he heard that advice? He had to find a way to protect his interests, and that's when the trouble began.

When I think about Ike all these years later, I'm trying to understand. The older I grow, and the longer I'm away from him, the more clearly I can see Ike. You can analyze a person when you have that kind of distance, and that's what I've been doing—looking for the reasons behind his behavior, trying to figure out where he was coming from, telling myself "Oh, *that's* why he did what he did."

Like me, many of Ike's struggles began at birth. He came from Clarksdale, Mississippi, angry and a fighter. When he was a boy, he watched his father die a slow, painful death after he was beaten mercilessly by white men who wanted to teach him a lesson for fooling around with a white woman. Ike held that hate deep inside him and never let it go.

When he was older, he had a hard time at school. Children were so cruel to him because he wasn't attractive. Girls would meet him *behind* the school building because he was fun to fool around with, but they refused to be seen with him in public. That led him to feel even more anger and hate. Success would be his revenge. "One day I'll have a big car, and all the women I want," he promised himself. He would do anything to get that.

The more time I spent with Ike, and saw how he behaved offstage, it was clear to me that he wasn't schooled properly. I knew the difference because the schools I'd attended had intelligent teachers and students from good homes. I was bussed in (I was orphaned at the time—I say that because my parents were gone and I was living with my grandparents or the Hendersons), but I was surrounded by educated people and I had the good sense to watch them.

When I was in school, I never wasted a minute. I sang in the choir. I played on the basketball team. I was a cheerleader. There was something I had that the teachers liked. They always took me under their wing in some way. And if they offered me advice, I listened. The school librarian told me to hold in my stomach for better posture, and I've been doing that my whole life. The principal said he expected good behavior from me, and I vowed not to disappoint him. I wanted to know the better way to do things, so I could improve myself and grow.

Ike never had that opportunity. I don't think he finished grade school, and even when he knew what he was talking about, he sounded ignorant, which gave him a complex about the way he spoke. A lot of his fight came from the fact that he was embarrassed about his lack of education and his poor manners.

Ike was very smart in other ways, though: he was what we called *street-smart*, and he had tremendous musical talent. Thanks to his magic on the guitar and the piano (and his fierce ambition) Ike got himself the big car, the big house, and all the women he could ever want. And he got one hit record. Then he stalled, and when he thought he wasn't going to get more than that, the anger and frustration came back.

When "A Fool in Love" looked like it would be a hit, Ike had a brainstorm: he turned the Kings of Rhythm into the Ike and Tina Turner Revue, a new act that was supposed to give us a chance to appeal to a broader audience. But, if the new revue worked, and we *were* successful, Ike needed to control me, to own me, economically and psychologically, so I could never leave him. The economic part was easily accomplished. Ike wasn't a singer. He wanted to be a star, but the only way he could do it was through me. So, he said to himself, "Okay, I'll change her name and call the group the Ike and Tina Turner Revue—that puts me right there in the title, so she doesn't exist without me." My new first name rhymed with "Sheena," a character he remembered from a television series. And "Turner," my new last name, implied that we were married (which, of course, we weren't). Ike always had a strategy. He actually registered a trademark on the name "Tina Turner" so it belonged to him, not me.

What's in a name? Everything. With those two words, I became Ike's property.

To control me psychologically, Ike worked several angles. Before our relationship became sexual, he preyed on my better nature by begging me to be loyal to him. In his hangdog way, he told me that every time he wrote a song for someone, if it became a hit, they left him. I was grateful for everything he did for me—if Ike liked you, he would give you the shirt off his back—so I promised him that I was different, that he could trust me, that I would never, ever, leave him. As long as I can remember, I was always honest and never told lies. It was just my way. When I said something, I meant it. A promise was a promise, and that was it. My promise to Ike meant something to me and I intended to keep it.

———

But Ike didn't trust me. Actually, Ike didn't trust anyone. Just in case I changed my mind, and decided not to honor my promise, he wanted insurance, so he found another way to keep me tied to him: fear. When he proposed the new Ike and Tina Turner idea, claiming that I needed a better stage name, my instincts told me I was moving into something that wasn't going to be good. I didn't know better then. I dared to question him and said I didn't want to change my name and wasn't sure I wanted to go out on tour, which was his plan. First, he was verbally abusive. Ike had a nasty tongue and I was hearing the worst of it. Then he picked up a wooden shoe stretcher and came toward, me, intending to teach me a lesson I wouldn't soon forget.

Ike knew exactly what he was doing. If you play guitar, your hands are your most valuable asset, so you never use your fists in a fight. He protected his hands and used the shoe stretcher to strike me in the head—always the head, I learned through experience—and it really hurt. I was so shocked I started to cry. My mother and father fought constantly, but I'd never seen a man beat a woman so violently. This was new to me, and I was still trying to figure out what was happening. I never, ever, expected what came next. Ike put down the stretcher and ordered me to get on the bed. That was really awful. I hated him at that moment. The very last thing I wanted to do was make love, if you could call it that. When he finished, I lay there with a swollen head, thinking, "You're pregnant and you have no place to go. You really have gotten yourself into something now." Tina Turner was born that night, and "Little Ann" disappeared forever.

In the early days of the Ike and Tina Turner Revue, it was Ike who behaved like the star. I was the Cinderella, the slave girl, really and truly. The revue consisted of me, Ike and the band, and the "Ikettes," three female singers who backed me onstage. I left baby Craig in St. Louis with a sitter, tucked my pregnancy bump behind a maternity girdle—I was skinny enough so that nothing showed—and hit the road for my first grueling, multicity tour.

You can't imagine the condition of the clubs we played in those early days—especially the black clubs. They didn't have proper dressing rooms. We were lucky if there was a storage room or a closet we could use to get ready, and we usually had to clean it first. We sat on our little Samsonite suitcases, or on a keg instead of chairs, and we set up our own mirrors, hoping there was a light, even a bare bulb, so we could see to put on our makeup. As for toilets—there were none. We'd use a cut-off bottle, then walk outside to throw it away. Later, once we graduated into some of the white clubs, the conditions were a little better, but not much.

Ike was so cheap that we had to do everything ourselves. And he was strict! For someone who was so reckless and self-indulgent in his personal life, Ike insisted on controlling everything that had to do with the revue. He fined the musicians and the dancers for the smallest infractions. A torn stocking, a late arrival to a rehearsal, or a defiant word would arouse his ire, and he'd slap the offender with a ten-dollar fine. One rebellious Ikette complained that she ended up owing Ike more money than she made. Someone asked me if I got fined for breaking a rule (meaning, did I get preferential treatment?). That was a joke. I didn't get fined because I didn't get *paid*. I just got shelter, food, and some pretty things on the rare occasion when Ike was feeling generous.

That's why I never became a prima donna. I came from a time

———

when nothing was given to me. My philosophy was, never complain when things get tough—or tougher—just accept it, and keep going. Deal with what you have—good or bad—and find a way to make it work.

The Ikettes and I always tried to make the best of it, and we had fun together. We were on the road so much that our companionship was the only life we had. We were like sisters. Robbie Montgomery, who was one of the original Ikettes (and is now best known as the founder of the popular soul food restaurant Sweetie Pie's) used to lend me money because she knew Ike never paid me. It meant so much to me to know I could always depend on her.

I loved dancing with the girls, and sometimes it was my only pleasure. We rehearsed constantly—even in the car traveling from one show to another—and we worked hard on our choreography, making up steps or taking steps and making them our own. (*Sham, Ba, Ba, Ba, Ba, Freeze, Freeze, Turn! You go up, I come back.*) The Pony, our signature footwork, came from—I don't remember where exactly—but it was meant to mimic a pony when a lady rides it. You know, the lady sits, and the pony does this and that with his legs, prancing. For us, the Pony was a traveling step—it kept us moving back and forth across the stage, like Michael Jackson did much later with his Moonwalk. We really enjoyed it when Ike had the music going fast. We'd say, "Oh, ho, it's on the track tonight." I mean, you had to be a great dancer to move that quickly, and we had a good time showing off our talents to the audience.

We also loved planning our "look." Through trial and error, we learned to wear costumes that emphasized movement and called attention to our legs, the shorter the better. Maintaining a hairstyle on the road was always a problem, especially without a proper dressing room. Even as a child, I had a complicated relationship with my hair. I pulled my braids out because my hair was woolly and big and didn't want to be contained. When I got older, I had it straightened, which meant spending hours at a salon, dripping with harsh chemicals, while a beautician tugged and tugged to get rid of the kinks. All that time spent on processing was futile. With black hair, if you're singing, dancing, and sweating, when you reach up to touch your head, it springs right back, natural again.

It took an accident, one that turned out to be a blessing in disguise, to prompt me to get my first wig. I was at a hair salon with the Ikettes and the beautician let the bleach stay on my head a little too long. My overprocessed hair started to break and fall out, and it was a disaster because I had a show that night! There was no choice but to hide the damage under a wig. The wig was a lifesaver, but more than that, I loved the way it looked, how the hair moved when I moved, how it was straight and pretty and held a style, no matter what I did.

This happened in the early 1960s, when wigs were primitive, with hair that was full, heavy, and blunt. I didn't want to look like I was wearing a curtain of fake hair, so I taught myself how to customize the wigs to appear natural. I started by thinning the hair in certain places, the first step in making it look right. Then, I took a needle and sewed on wefts, small pieces of extra hair, positioning them wherever I thought volume was needed. I bought high-quality hair, and eventually, with careful sculpting and styling, my wigs were the best in the business. We'd wear them onstage, wash and set them after the show, and they were ready to go the next day.

Ike left all of those details to me, but he controlled the music.

Even though I was fairly new to the business of performing, I had my own ideas about how to use my voice. There was music I wanted to sing, and music I didn't want to sing. For example, I've never been a jazz person. I grew up on country-western music, and when I got older, I liked listening to great singers like Faye Adams and LaVern Baker. I especially loved Baker's hit, "Tweedle Dee." I also liked listening to Mahalia Jackson and Sister Rosetta Tharpe. Gospel singers could really sing! And they had so much personality and presence.

I didn't have a typical "girl" voice, so I was also inspired by some of the male singers who were popular at the time. My absolute favorite was Sam Cooke. I had the good fortune to see him perform at the Howard Theater in Washington, D.C., in 1960. He was the prettiest black man I'd ever seen besides Harry, my first boyfriend in high school.

I went to his show with one of the Ikettes, and the place was packed. Sam Cooke was standing there singing—his shirt was open and he was wearing a beautifully tailored, continental suit. He never put chemicals in his hair—it was just natural. He was singing *"Darling, you send me,"* and he was so cool and absolutely wonderful. I was so mesmerized. I found myself walking to the stage until the girl I was with started pulling at me, saying, "Bullock [they called me Bullock], I will kill you! What are you doing?" The place was going crazy. Sam Cooke was the first performer I saw who had that effect on an audience. They just melted at the sound of his voice.

I finally had the opportunity to meet him a couple of years later at a hotel in Miami. We were all at the pool, and he came over to talk to me. I was surprised that Sam Cooke even knew me—actually, I'm not sure if he knew who I was—maybe he was just being kind. You know how some people can see if you're sad? I was very sad at the time, probably because Ike was up to no good, and the fact that Sam Cooke took the time to pay attention to me was very special. A short time later, I heard that he passed away. Ike gave me the bad news that he had been murdered. I was so happy that we had that moment together, and I still think about him and his beautiful voice.

I loved Ray Charles. He really knew how to rock the house when he sang "What'd I Say" with the Raelettes. As soon as he came out onstage, the place would jump up and start dancing and kicking. He had another kind of "soul." It wasn't traditional church soul. What he had, he brought with him on the planet. Ray Charles was an original.

So many of the black singers at the time were creative in their own way. Otis Redding, he was a suffering one with songs like "The Dock of the Bay." And James Brown—I remember seeing him at the Apollo. He came out with his little bow legs and did the Mashed Potato (which I took from him), and the audience went nuts. I'd never seen a black man in a light green jacket. He made quite the impression on me, and everyone else. He really had the people at his feet.

Each one of these acts I'm telling you about had something special. This is why the white people who came to their performances never went back to pop music. They liked what the black people were doing, and eventually, the sound crossed over into other kinds of music.

While I was listening to these musical greats, I was developing a sense of my own style, and I didn't like how Ike wanted me to sing. He favored a delivery that was almost like preaching, all that "Hey, Hey, Heying" and growling. I wanted to really *sing*, to be more expressive, more melodic, but I wasn't allowed to use my voice the way *I* wanted.

———

Looking back, I realize a lot of the fights I had with Ike happened because I disagreed with the way he wanted me to perform. We had what they call "artistic differences." I couldn't come right out and say to him, "I don't like that song," or "I don't want to deliver it this way." But he was smart. He could read my body language and see how I felt, and he didn't like being contradicted. "Miss Bullock," he'd say in an angry and patronizing voice. "Get out there and sing the song." One night, he actually spit at me when I dared to express my opinion.

There wasn't much time to think about how life *should* have been. Ike kept us too busy for that. Our schedule was fast and punishing, an endless loop of traveling, rehearsing, and performing, with on-the-fly recording sessions taking up any free time. The most exciting destination for me was New York City, when we played the Apollo Theater in August 1960. I remember driving over an enormous bridge. I took one look at the skyline and yelled, "New York!" Oh, the beauty that was New York at the time. The sun was even more yellow than yellow. I didn't know the names of the streets, but I'd never seen such buildings—they were like stretching up to God—high, high, high! The skyscrapers with their gleaming windows, the sounds of the horns, the ladies dressed up in their high heels (not sneakers, like today), scarves, and white gloves, the hot dogs from the little carts on the street—New York had it all. Seeing it firsthand was an exceptional experience, just like watching a movie, and one I would *never* forget.

We had a lively audience at the Apollo and we were in great company. A young Flip Wilson was the comic that night. Ike was uneasy during the show because I was moving around so much and I was in an advanced state of pregnancy. He tried to rein me in, saying, "You'd better stop doing this or doing that," but I twisted and did the Pony right up until I gave birth in October. My dresses were designed to hide the baby, which was not easy to do because I was carrying a boy and my belly was pointed (just like the old wives used to say at the time). I wore a tight, straight underdress that held everything in, with a loose chiffon layer on top to camouflage the "bump." I was so young that I had boundless energy and stamina. I felt wonderful the whole time I was pregnant.

I don't know what came over me, whether it was the thrill of being in that theater, or the excitement of all the attention, but at one point during our Apollo performance, when the music was moving really fast, I jumped off the stage and into the pit. Thanks to my clever costuming, I didn't look like I was in my eighth month, which was a good thing. I think people would have been *really* nervous about that! But the baby was never in danger. Honestly, it wasn't that big a drop and I was a good athlete. I knew that I could handle it.

On our return trip cross-country, we passed through St. Louis to check on Craig, who was still living with a sitter at Ike's house. It broke my heart to see him. He was so little that he barely knew how to talk. All my son wanted was to sit in my lap and be held, but Ike wouldn't let him. He thought that was being a sissy or something. Later, I found Craig in his bed, in a puddle of water from crying. I took him in my arms and tried to console him. The next day, after we left, he was running around, calling "Ann, Ann," looking for me. He remembered the love of his mother. Every time she left him, he always missed her. He missed Ann. I missed Ann, too, the girl I used to be before Ike made life so complicated.

4

"I DON'T WANNA FIGHT"

" We must stop pretending

I can't live this lie **"**

Our crazy touring routine left no time for family life. I almost gave birth to our son, Ronnie, while we were still on that first tour. Luckily, Ike noticed that I was about to deliver and rerouted us to a hospital in Los Angeles, where we were booked at some clubs. He expected me to have the baby and bounce right back. Two days after becoming a mother, I was onstage, singing and dancing as if nothing had happened. The reality was, if I didn't sing, there was no show, and no show meant no money.

Whenever I think of this, I'm completely puzzled. Why, I wonder, didn't Ike treat me better? That sounds just like one of Ike's songs, but it was true. He couldn't have been thinking rationally. If he had been kind to me, if he'd been caring and respectful, I would have *wanted* to stay. Wouldn't that have made sense? I could have loved him. I did at first. And if we had collaborated in a more professional way, we might have had the success that was so important to him, like Mickey & Sylvia, a popular duo at the time. But Ike was always his own worst enemy. He destroyed anything that was good. He just couldn't help himself.

I see now that our life together was a mockery of a "normal" relationship: defined by abuse and fear, not love, or even affection. We went through the motions of doing all the things happy couples did. We had a child together. Ike moved us to Los Angeles and rented a house, where we lived with our two families in a Brady Bunch way, with Ike Jr. and Michael, Ike's sons by Lorraine, growing up alongside Craig and Ronnie. I was "Mother" to the four boys—ranging in age from two to four, when I was only twenty-three. Then, in 1962, we got married in that depressing civil ceremony in Tijuana.

In L.A., we were living in a beautiful place, with perfect weather, blues skies, and palm trees. But there was no peace in Ike's world. He insisted on putting a recording studio in the living room, and on the rare occasion when we were in town, he worked all hours of the night. I couldn't stay up like that. Gosh, they would have taken me to the hospital. Sometimes he'd look at me coldly and say in all seriousness, "Tell me, what do you do for me?" I wanted to answer, "*Everything*— singing, cooking, cleaning, and anything else around here that I have to do"—but I kept quiet, all the while thinking, *How will I survive this?*

Home was often unpleasant, but being on the road presented problems, too. We were away from the house more than we were there, which was never good for the children, and I did suffer about that. Ike kept us so busy after our first tour that we had bookings in between our bookings. Usually, the musicians rode on our bus, while we (Ike, me, and probably a mistress) followed in Ike's Cadillac Brougham, which was outfitted with a safe in the trunk.

Traveling was wonderful when it took me to exotic places I'd never imagined seeing, like New York and London. When I was growing up, the only time we left home was to visit relatives, and most of my family lived nearby, so it was never much of a trip. Our circle was so small that when my mother ran away, my father was able to figure out where she was hiding on the basis of who she knew, narrowing it down to relatives in Chicago, Detroit, or St. Louis, where he ultimately found her. With the Ike and Tina Turner Revue, however, I had the amazing opportunity to see the world. I never had time to be a tourist, to go sightseeing or to visit museums, because Ike worked us too hard to do anything like that. But I watched people and saw how they lived, and I learned from them.

There was one part of the world I would have been happy to skip. During the 1960s, it was very hard for us to travel in the Deep South because we were likely to run into dangerous racial situations. I can't tell you how many times I witnessed *this* conversation: We'd be driving through Mississippi, let's say, when a white police officer would see our black faces and signal the car to pull over. "Hey, boy," he'd say provocatively to Jimmy Thomas, one of our singers who doubled as a driver. "Doing a little speeding here, weren't you?" Jimmy would answer, "No, sir, I was doing the speed limit," as politely as possible. Then, the game of cat and mouse would begin.

The officer would respond, "That's not what I read on my meter. I think I have to take you in."

This would be Jimmy's cue to say, "Sir, you know, we're singers and we're a little bit late. Can we take care of this with you?"

Inevitably, money changed hands. The police officer drove away a little richer. And we were free to drive to our next job . . . until the next time we got pulled over. There was one instance when Jimmy, a master negotiator who could outtalk anyone, had me and Ike get out of the car to sing so we could convince the police that we really were entertainers on our way to a show.

When Rhonda started working for us in 1964, we had to be extra careful on Southern roads because the sight of a white woman traveling with a black band was guaranteed to attract attention and hostility. If we had a white bus driver, or guitar player, as we sometimes did, he and Rhonda would sit together. Once, when we needed gas in a particularly unwelcoming place, Rhonda had to get down on the floor of the car and we tossed coats and blankets over her so no one could see her when we pulled up to the pump.

Driving was tense, but eating in a restaurant, unless it was located on the black side of town, was like walking through a minefield. There was always the possibility that a simple meal could turn into a dangerous confrontation. I remember one time when we were in a diner, we sat down and ordered, but the waitress called the police just because our group was black. Then she started yelling, calling me a "black bitch." I jumped up; Ike was trying to hold me back, and I said very clearly, "But I'm a pretty black bitch," which made me feel better. A lot of times, after finishing a late show, we sidestepped the problem by eating at a Greyhound bus terminal, where we wouldn't attract attention. It was safer, but the food wasn't very appetizing.

If we weren't doing a gig on the fly, which meant there was no time to sleep between venues, we booked rooms at hotel and motel chains, and we always had telegrams confirming our reservations. In the old days, when you pulled up to a Holiday Inn, the empty rooms had windows with open curtains and a lamp in the center, so you could actually see how busy it was. But some nights, we walked into a hotel that looked empty, reservations in hand, only to be told that the place was suddenly "full" and we were turned away. The truth was, they didn't want blacks, especially black musicians, checking in.

Rhonda, who was a feisty young woman, refused to take no for an answer. Sometimes she would walk into the hotel alone to check in, then the rest of us would follow. Eventually, she called someone at the head office to explain what was going on—that we were experiencing discrimination at some of their locations. Moving forward, our reservations were honored, or, thanks to Rhonda, the hotel manager would find himself in serious trouble with the boss.

There were a few times when our schedule was so crazy that there was nowhere to stop, so we'd stay in the car or on the bus. In the summer, it was wonderful to sleep outside on the grass. We did all that kind of stuff—anything to get by and make it to the next show. Traveling became a way of life.

Whether we were on the road or back in L.A.—by this time Ike had bought a house on Olympiad Drive in the suburb of View Park—Ike's strategy was to keep me close to him, to make me feel small. If he forced me to stay in the "Ike and Tina" bubble, surrounded by his narrow circle of his people—I wouldn't know the outside world, or my place in it. In 1966, the opportunity to record "River Deep—Mountain High" came into my life when I needed it the most. I can't describe how special I felt when Phil Spector, the legendary record producer, contacted Ike about wanting to work with me. I didn't know much about him, but the fact that someone other than Ike believed in me made me feel wonderful. Of course, Ike's attitude at first was "No way," until he realized this was another opportunity to use me to make money. He was always like that when it came to me—just like a pimp. Not the kind who worked on the streets, but a pimp nonetheless. Ike said something like "Pay me first" to Phil, and got twenty thousand dollars for a loan-out. But Phil was smart. He wanted no part of Ike or the trouble that came with him. Just Tina. Phil insisted that I come alone to his house in Hollywood so we could start working on the song together.

I was excited about trying new music and maybe a different style of singing. I rarely had a chance to go anywhere alone in those days, and I was determined to make the most of my freedom. I dressed carefully for the occasion. I think I always had an instinct for picking out clothes, and this was a good moment for me. The miniskirts and bell bottoms that were so popular at the time were perfect for my skinny frame. I wore a white jacket with matching pants and I had long, straight hair courtesy of one of my terrific Tina wigs.

Phil's mansion was tucked away on La Collina Drive, off Sunset. A little nervous because I didn't know what to expect, I followed a private road that led into a courtyard with a large fountain. I knocked at the door, but no one answered. I pushed it open and walked into a really big room decorated in the style of old Hollywood, with a winding staircase and old-fashioned, oversized European furniture. *Wow, this is weird*, I thought to myself, because I was still all alone. I was startled by a voice—not a person, it turned out, but a talking mynah bird, who kept shrieking, "Someone's here!" It was a down-the-rabbit-hole moment right out of *Alice in Wonderland*, and I was Alice.

I found a seat and waited, crossing and uncrossing my legs, while the chatty mynah bird continued its conversation with itself. I hadn't had any contact with Phil—Ike had made all the arrangements—but when he came bounding down the staircase, I realized that I had seen this leprechaun-like man hanging out at the clubs where we performed. He was always tucked away in a corner, wearing a funny cap. There was no cap that day—just an untamed corona of crinkly hair, which stuck out in all directions and reminded me of the mad scientists in the horror movies I loved to watch. He was dressed boyishly in a T-shirt and jeans, and his bare feet struck me as being very, very white. He introduced himself politely, "Hello, Tina, I'm Phil Spector," and he sounded intelligent.

We walked over to the grand piano in the living room, where he sat down to play "River Deep—Mountain High," the song he had in mind for me. When he signaled that I should sing, I immediately started screaming the lyrics à la Ike—*"When I was a little girl I had a rag doll"*—thinking this was what he wanted to hear. I gave him full-on Tina, loud and lusty, but Phil interrupted me right away and said, "No, no, not like that—just the melody." *Just the melody?* I thought, *Oh, oh, this is really wonderful!* I feel it even now, how exhilarating it was to be given permission to use my voice in a new way. I wanted to run and jump in the air and shout "Woo hoo!"

Working with Phil was a musical education. Every time I went there to rehearse, he'd say the same thing, carefully stripping away all traces of Ike from my performance. Phil had a sound in his head. He was very strict about sticking to the melody and told me to sing it exactly the way he imagined—no improvising, not a note.

That sound was so haunting, but the funny thing was that as soon as I left Phil, I couldn't remember a single bar of the song. I knew Ike wouldn't like it—and I was afraid he might punish me with a beating, the way he usually did when something made him unhappy—so I probably pushed it out of my brain. The melody was so different from anything I'd done before that I just couldn't hold it in my head . . . until one weekend when Ike and I were driving back from a club date. Suddenly, the lyrics came to me in a rush and I started singing: "And I'll love you just the way I loved that rag doll," Phil's way, melodically. Ike was listening impassively. Just as I thought, what he heard was not his style at all.

"So that's it, huh," he said, dismissing it. Even as he spoke, I knew he was thinking of how he could change the vocals to be more "Ike and Tina," which would have destroyed it. But he was stuck. This was a Phil Spector production, start to finish. Ike had been paid all that money and there was nothing he could do.

The more time I spent with Phil, the more I realized that he was unusual, to say the least. He did a few things that struck me as being downright strange . . . like the time he picked up an apple from a dirty ashtray and ate it. I couldn't understand why he did that, you know, it was covered with ashes. I dismissed it thinking, *Oh, he's so busy at the studio.* We were all a little crazy from exhaustion, working long hours trying to get that song right. What I didn't get at the time was that Phil was *always* a little nuts.

Day after day, we met at the Gold Star Studio, where Phil was spending more money on one song than most producers spent on an entire album. I sang the opening line a thousand times before we moved on to "And it gets stronger every day," working so hard to satisfy Phil. I honestly couldn't tell the difference between when I did it wrong and when I did it right. You know, sometimes I'm a bit naïve. I was hot, covered with sweat, and all I could think of was that I needed to be more comfortable. "Do you mind if I take my top off?" I asked. In the middle of the take, without missing a beat, I ripped off my blouse and kept singing. Well, I had a bra on, but the reaction in the studio was bigger than *Ben-Hur. Tina took off her blouse!* I thought, you know, whatever it takes to sing that song. I still don't know what he wanted. I still don't know if I pleased him. But I never stopped trying.

The other thing I was naïve about was the "Wall of Sound." I didn't know a thing about Phil Spector's "wall." Ike never discussed music with me. I went into the studio one day and I was surprised to find a whole orchestra and a choir, yes, a *choir*, of backup singers. I was just a girl from Tennessee who got caught up with Ike and became a singer. Never, ever had I seen anything like this, except in a movie. Phil said, "Okay, Tina?" I tried not to look nervous. I went into the booth and started singing, and there I was at the center of the Wall of Sound—the strings, the horns, the snare drums. My voice was one of the instruments.

"River Deep—Mountain High" is a particularly difficult song to sing, and according to Phil, no one else had been able to get it right—not Darlene Love or the Ronettes, despite their terrific voices. I think he chose me because most singers have to go into falsetto when they hit high notes. But I can sing octaves higher—and stand up to an orchestra—in my natural speaking voice. Phil had watched me night after night at the club. He knew what my voice could do, and he decided I would be the one to bring his song to life. Before that, I was singing Ike's way, because that's how I started and that's how I was produced. But I always knew I had another talent. I knew it was there and I wanted to explore it. This song opened my eyes to possibilities. I felt liberated, excited, ready to challenge myself vocally with other kinds of songs. To this day, I have never done a live show without singing it. The audience wouldn't stand for that.

"River Deep—Mountain High" was supposed to be a hit for us, but, surprisingly, America rejected it. The deejays were puzzled about how to play it: if pressed, they said it wasn't "black" enough to be rhythm and blues, or "white" enough to be pop. England was another story. There, the song was a sensation. It went straight to the top of the charts, and an exciting new group, the Rolling Stones, decided that they wanted the Ike and Tina Turner Revue to be the opening act on their upcoming tour in the UK.

If "River Deep—Mountain High" introduced me to the way I wanted to sing, our first trip to Europe showed me exactly how I wanted to *live*. In 1966, London was the center of the universe, the place where everything went "Pop!" and the home of "mods and rockers" and Carnaby Street. At times, I felt that I was in the middle of a fairy tale. I loved the double-decker buses, the little black cabs, and the pretty white town houses that lined the streets. We stayed at the Norfolk Hotel near the Cromwell Road, and every morning at 6 a.m. we were awakened by the sound of horses clomping their way to the Changing of the Guard at Buckingham Palace. The show got out so late that Wimpy's, the English version of McDonald's, was the only place open, but somehow it seemed more colorful than our fast-food places at home. Even the hamburgers were charming in London, although when we tried to order iced tea the Brits thought we were crazy. "You want hot tea and then you want ice in it? That's an American for you," they said dismissively.

For a girl coming from Nutbush and St. Louis, it was like being transported to another world. I felt an immediate connection with the city and its people, like love at first sight. Then, *even* then, I didn't want to go back to America. I wanted to stay! I felt the same way when I saw France and Germany for the first time. Somehow, these faraway places seemed like home, and maybe they were in another life. I'm a big believer in reincarnation.

Playing the Royal Albert Hall with the Stones was both thrilling and terrifying, given that the room held over five thousand seats and was completely packed because everyone wanted to see the Rolling Stones. We'd never performed for such a big audience. Ike looked out from behind the curtain and said, "I want Ike and Tina, just Ike and

Tina, to fill this place," which sounded like a pipe dream. We were a little nervous, but needlessly so. The crowd loved us, and so did the Stones. We blew them away with our dancing. Mick said that we raised the temperature of the room, really got the audience going, so by the time the Stones came out, they felt like they had to work harder to top us. That's a true collaboration, when the opening act and the lead band play off each other and create a new energy.

As usual, "Cinderella" had a hundred responsibilities, so I spent most of my time backstage at the Albert Hall, prepping for our performance. When I finally saw Mick Jagger for the first time, he was standing in the wings, and what I noticed about him was that he had the whitest face. Later, he showed up at the dressing room I shared with the Ikettes and said in his unmistakable voice, "I like how you girls dance." We'd seen him strutting with his tambourine onstage, and he was a little awkward back then. We thought it was kind of cute that he admired our dancing, so we pulled him into our group and taught him how to do the Pony. Mick caught on fast, but he found it difficult to do certain steps. That didn't keep him from trying, and when we watched him doing a little bit of it during his next show we thought, *Well, that's good*. Not that he ever gave me and the girls credit for his fancy new footwork. To this day, Mick likes to say, "My mother taught me how to dance." And I say, "Okay. That's fine." But I know better.

While we were in England, I went to see a psychic, which was the beginning of a lifelong passion for me. I'm always looking for guidance. At the end of that first reading, the psychic told me something I'd never expected to hear. She said, "You will be among the biggest of stars. A partner of yours will fall, like a leaf from a tree in autumn, but you will survive and go on." I didn't believe it was possible that there could be a Tina without Ike. Still, I tucked the idea in the back of my mind and thought about it when times were rough. And they were getting rougher every day.

Living with Ike was a high-wire act. I had to tread carefully, watching what I said, or how I looked at him. He was always on edge, ready to fight like he was a dog; once you unchained him, he'd jump on anything, just to fight. I had no other place to go and no money of my own, not even a five-dollar allowance. When I wanted cash, I was reduced to sneaking a few bills from the roll Ike kept in his wallet. If he was in a good mood, he'd arrange for me to go shopping, but that was because, in his mind, when other people thought I looked good, it made *him* look good. In a perverse way, the bruises he gave me—the black eye, the busted lip or rib, the swollen nose—were markings, a sign of ownership, another way of Ike saying, "She's mine and I can do whatever I want with her."

I knew it was time to leave, but I didn't know how to take the first step. The one time I tried to run away, I failed miserably. I had nowhere to go so I boarded a bus to St. Louis to see Muh. It didn't take Ike very long to figure out where I was headed, and he caught up with me at a bus stop on the way and ordered me to come back. That didn't go well. At my lowest, I convinced myself that death was my only way out. And I was fine with going because I just didn't see the point of living that life any longer. I actually tried to kill myself. Why did I snap on an ordinary day in 1968? For starters, there were three women at the house at the time, and Ike was having sex with all of them. Three of us were named Ann. You can't make stuff like that up. He only had to remember one name.

One of the "Anns," Ann Thomas, was pregnant with his child,

another insult to me. I felt so bad that I was surrounded by all of those women. I knew they were Ike's girlfriends—everyone knew—but there was nothing I could do about it. Even Rhonda, our biggest fan and a vital part of the Ike and Tina Turner operation, had an obligatory affair with Ike, one that she came to regret. He seduced every woman in our circle. That's what he did. In his mind, sex was power. When a woman became his conquest, he believed he owned her.

To be honest, sometimes his girlfriends, like Rhonda, became my closest friends because, in a funny way, we were in the same boat, dependent on Ike, constantly at his beck and call, *ruled* by him, abused by him. We were like members of a cult. What do you call them? Sisterwives?

But wasn't I supposed to be the *real* wife? A little more elevated than the others? It was just the opposite. Ike actually treated me worse than his girlfriends. I was just a singer: someone to use and sweep under the rug. Everything was diminishing—my status, my confidence, my world. I was growing older, maybe more introspective, and out of my unhappiness came thoughts of suicide, so I hatched a plan. I went to my doctor and told him I was having trouble sleeping. I might have even said that Ike was the one who needed sleeping pills. He was a good doctor—he warned me that the pills were dangerous, that I shouldn't take too many. I pretended to listen, then went home and put them away, ready for whenever I decided I'd had enough.

For no particular reason, *this* turned out to be the night I'd had enough. I wasn't thinking about the kids—I wasn't thinking at all. It felt like something I *had* to do. Right after dinner, I took the pills, all fifty of them, which is not an easy thing to do. I knew they would take time to work, in fact I was counting on it. If I could just make it to the stage for our opening number, Ike would still get paid for the booking. That's how our contract worked. If I got sick *before* the show started, it was considered a cancellation and there would be no money. I was so well trained that even my suicide had to be convenient for Ike. I managed to get to the club where we were performing, a place called the Apartment, and started to put on my makeup, struggling to appear normal.

The Ikettes were running around, fussing with their wigs and dresses, the usual preshow rush of activity—when someone noticed I wasn't right. I had drawn a line across my face with my eyebrow pencil and I was having trouble speaking. Panicked, they ran for Rhonda, who took one look at me and called Ike to come right away.

I don't remember any of this, but I'm told that Rhonda and Ike threw me into the car and rushed me to the nearest hospital. If there's a crisis, Rhonda's the person you want at the wheel. She's fearless and has nerves of steel, which she needed that night because they had to take me to several hospitals before they found one with an emergency room. Rhonda was speeding through stop signs and running red lights the whole way, certain they were going to lose me. Meanwhile, Ike was in the back, trying to wake me up. He was so desperate that he stuck his finger down my throat to force me to throw up. I can imagine what was going through his mind, *Don't let her die, don't let her die,* thinking of the money I pulled in, something he would never admit to me.

At Daniel Freeman Hospital, the emergency room doctors took over. They pumped my stomach, but couldn't get me to respond. I was still out cold. Ike asked, "Can I talk to her?" At that point, they were willing to try anything. He moved close to me, probably doing his best imitation of a concerned husband, and started speaking. My subconscious mind heard him—a familiar voice, something I woke up with, slept with, lived with, the voice of my tormentor, a hell voice, cursing me softly. Of course, he got through. Immediately, my heart started racing.

They said, "Keep talking. We have a pulse."

The next thing I remember, I woke up and was trying to figure out why I was in a hospital bed. The nurse came in and said, "Hello, can you tell me your name?"

"I'm Tina Turner," I slurred.

"Oh, can you sing?" she asked.

"Yeah, I can sing," and I belted, *When I was a little girl . . . ,*" the opening line from "River Deep—Mountain High." Interesting that even when I was semiconscious, I made the decision *not* to sing one of Ike's songs.

I fell asleep again. The next day, I woke up, turned my head, and looked right into the face of Ike.

"You should die, you motherfucker," he said.

My first thought was, *I didn't escape this.* I looked at him and said, "Oh no." Then I looked away. He knew that I had taken the pills because of him, and that was it. He came to visit just the one time and didn't come back. Didn't even care. The only thing he cared about was the show. As soon as I was released from the hospital, he forced me to go back to work. That night, I was weak and had terrible stomach cramps, yet I had to get onstage and sing and dance—had to go through the whole show with energy and a smile on my face.

When we finished, the Ikettes held me up and helped me to the dressing room. There was Ike, fuming.

"You should die, motherfucker," he said again. "But if you die," he added, "you know what you would do to me."

It didn't make sense, him telling me that I should die, but if I did, it would be bad for him. But nothing made sense in those days. Ike was on an ego trip of "I, me, mine." It was always about him. Always.

As terrible as the experience was—and I felt sick for a long time—I learned something. My suicide attempt wasn't a classic cry for attention, or help. When I took those pills, I chose death, and I chose it honestly. I was unhappy when I woke up. But I never tried it again because I made an important realization, one that changed the course of my life. I came out of the darkness believing that I was meant to survive. I was here for a reason.

I knew now that there was only one way out of this nightmare, and it was through the door.

5

"A CHANGE IS GONNA COME"

" There have been times that I thought I couldn't last for long

But now I think I'm able to carry on "

In describing my life, a journalist once said that my experiences with Ike were "Dantesque." I probably didn't understand it at the time, but now that I've actually read Dante, I know what he meant: I went through Hell, literally. In *The Divine Comedy*, Dante travels through Hell and Purgatory before finally reaching Paradise. There's a lot of poetry along the way, but the basic journey is one from pain to peace, from darkness to enlightenment. Ike lived in a world of darkness, and he tried to hold me prisoner there with him. It worked for a long time, but after my suicide attempt, something shifted. I spent the first seven years of my marriage wondering what I had gotten into, and the last seven trying to figure how to get out.

There were many levels of Hell, and I experienced them every day. For example, Ike never had any patience for illness. In 1969, after another tour with the Rolling Stones, I was so sick that I could barely hold up my head. I had to drive myself to the doctor, and to my horror, the only car available was Ike's limousine. I wasn't a good driver in a regular car, but a limousine? Somehow, I made it to the appointment, and the doctor took one look at me and said, "You're going to the hospital right from here." So I had to get back behind the wheel of that thing and drive to the ER. It turned out that I had TB. Ike was upset— not because I was sick, of course, but because I couldn't work and he had to cancel our upcoming dates. The Rolling Stones sweetly sent me flowers, but Ike didn't. I was in a hospital bed for several weeks, slowly recovering, and it never even occurred to him to visit me.

It gets worse.

While I was recuperating, Ike had the crazy idea to redecorate the house, with disastrous results. When we'd first moved into that house on Olympiad Drive, it was furnished with sensible pieces from the previous family. Nothing exciting, but the décor was simple and comfortable. Then Ike got his hands on the place when I wasn't looking and turned it into a hipster whorehouse.

Anyone who knows me understands that my surroundings are very important to me. My friends and I joke that I must have been an interior designer in another life. I want to live in an atmosphere of beauty and harmony, with candles, flowers, and classic furniture. I know exactly how I want a room to look, and I know how to bring that vision to life. I remember when I was a child living in a back room no bigger than a closet at my cousin's house in Tennessee. The space was ice-cold in the winter and hot and airless in the summer, yet I still took the time to dress it up with a proper bedspread and objects I considered treasures, because I wanted it to be nice.

Ike never let me express myself the whole time we were married. After I left him, I decorated my homes in England, Germany, France, and Switzerland, and each one had a beauty and personality all its own. I believe my sense of style comes naturally to me and is an extension of who I am. Unfortunately, Ike's style was an extension of who *he* was—a vulgar man with no taste—and I had to live with it.

Where did he even find such awful furniture? I wondered. The sofas had ugly metal prongs that looked suspiciously like spiky penises. The coffee table was shaped like an oversized guitar, while the television cabinet was supposed to look like a giant snail, or a whale, or something. The colors were garish, with swaths of red and gold everywhere. The bedroom was something that belonged in Las Vegas, with a mirror over the bed and curtains around it. The kitchen had green-and-white tiles that couldn't be cleaned easily—it took half a day to scrub that floor, and guess who ended up doing it? Bob Krasnow, a music producer, came to the house one day and was surprised to find me, the star of the Ike and Tina Turner Revue, with a scarf wrapped around my head, on my knees scrubbing. So much for the glamorous life of Tina Turner! Bob had a wicked sense of humor and wasn't afraid of offending Ike. "You mean you can actually spend seventy thousand dollars at Woolworth's?" was his assessment of Ike's dubious decorating talent.

Whenever I tried to improve the house, Ike got angry. I think he was so insecure about his taste and his choices (a throwback to his lack of education) that he lashed out at anyone who challenged him. If he noticed something was different, I would almost get trampled to the ground and he'd insist that I put it back exactly the way it was. One day, I tried changing the towels in the bathroom, and oh, he really cursed me out. "Get those fucking towels out of there and put back the ones that were here before," he yelled. This was over *towels*. There was no freedom to do anything. In his mind, I existed just to please him. The whole time I lived there we called it "the house"—we never called it "home." But it was the only home I had.

Success should have made things better. Ike and Tina were in demand, and we performed throughout the U.S., including at Madison Square Garden, and appeared on popular television shows such as *The Smothers Brothers Comedy Hour* and *The Andy Williams Show*.

But Ike was just as controlling and abusive onstage as he was at the house. He forced me to sing "I've Been Loving You Too Long" in such a cheap and sexual way that it became my least favorite song. I was embarrassed by the gestures I had to make at the microphone. If I did something he didn't want me to do, I'd hear about it, something as innocent as looking back at him while we were performing. If I did that, he'd say, "Turn around, motherfucker." I was practically in a trance, on automatic pilot, always thinking, *Ike is watching—you'd better just dance and sing.*

The first time I got a standing ovation, I didn't know what to do. We were in Paris in 1971. It was a really good show that night and the Parisians went crazy. They were standing up at their seats, clapping and calling for me. I asked Ike, "Can I go back onstage?" His anger was such that I had to make sure I didn't do anything that would get me a licking. I waited until he gave me permission. Even then, I was so overwhelmed by the applause, and so unaccustomed to the approval, that I said to the audience, "Do you mean it?" It was gratifying to hear them yell, "Yeah!" I was so thrilled that they liked me.

1971 was also the year that "Proud Mary" became a hit, and with its success, life took a downward turn. I heard the Creedence Clearwater Revival song by John Fogerty and suggested doing our own version. Ike and I played around with it for a while—we did that with new material—but I didn't know if, or when, we would actually do it onstage. Ike kept those decisions to himself. One night, when we were performing in Oakland, Ike started strumming the opening chords. I recognized the song, of course, but I wasn't prepared. I wasn't even certain if I remembered the words, so I started talking to buy a little time. "Every now and then I think you might like to hear something from us that's nice and easy," I improvised. "Every now and then" was an expression I used all the time (I still do). And then I added, "But there's just one thing. You see, we never ever do nothing nice and easy. We always do it nice . . . and rough." There was a bit of truth in my words because we always did everything so fast. Ike was still strumming, and then the words came back to me and I drifted into the slow version of the song, *"And we're rolling, rolling, rolling on a river."* People went crazy.

When I came up with the talking part, I was proud of myself like a rooster for making those lines up. Once Ike started playing the fast version, because dancing is in my genes, I just did something, *anything*, to give the audience something to look at. I don't even know what I did that first time. After the show, one of the Ikettes said, "Rolling on a river. Let's do what happens when you roll on a river," and we choreographed the movements to match the words.

"Proud Mary" climbed to number 4 on the pop charts and won the Grammy for Best R&B Vocal Performance by a Group. It was exactly the kind of mainstream success Ike had longed for, but it came with a price. The money from "Proud Mary" enabled Ike to fulfill his long-held dream of building his own sound studio, which was only a five-minute drive from the house. Acknowledging that I was the reason he finally got his studio, he named it after me—"Bolic," which was a nod to my maiden name, Bullock. It was an unusual gesture on his part. Most of the time, his brain didn't accept the fact that *anything* came from me.

Bolic Sound turned out to be Ike's downfall. He designed the studio to be a fortress, with locks on all the doors and security cameras that enabled him to watch what was going on in every room. There was rarely anything good going on there, especially late at night, when

Ike and his friends gathered to party. Ike would disappear into the studio and stay up for five nights at a time, maybe stopping to eat every now and then. Sometimes he just collapsed, and his mistress of the moment (one Ann or another) would help me roll his chair to the staircase, drag him up the steps, and put him to bed. He was just *out*. He'd sleep for about three days, until he gradually came back to life. His recovery routine never varied. He'd shower, shave, have his hair and nails done (probably by me), eat, and listen to the top radio station to see what music was out there, which would make him envious and drive him right back into the studio to work futilely on his own hit. Then the cycle would start again.

Sometimes, after these binges, I'd see a trace of the Ike I'd known when we first met. He'd say, "I'm sorry, Ann." But you know, so much damage had been done that all I could say was "Okay," and let it be. I knew he wouldn't be sorry for very long.

It got worse after Ike started doing cocaine. Someone told him the drug would give him more stamina for sex—as if Ike Turner needed to spend another minute on his sex life. Having sex was practically his full-time job. An interviewer once asked me how I felt about sex with Ike (which was actually a pretty forward question, now that I think of it). Was it all that? she wanted to know. I answered candidly. I really didn't like Ike's body, but I acknowledged that he was "blessed," so to speak, when it came to being endowed. Did that make him a good lover? "What can you do except go up and down, or sideways, or whatever it is that you do with sex?" I told her. I wanted affection. I wanted *romance*. I would have settled for common decency and respect. Sex with Ike had become an expression of hostility—a kind of rape—especially when it began or ended with a beating.

To this day, I question what really happened to Ike. Is that what drugs do? I wondered. I can't answer that question because I never, ever did drugs. I've certainly never been tempted to put anything up my nose. I watched Ike and his friends get crazy from the cocaine. His habit cost thousands of dollars a week to support and ended up burning a hole through his nostril, leaving him in constant pain that required even *more* cocaine to numb it. It was a vicious circle of substance abuse. On top of that, he was hooked on peach brandy. The combination was lethal. What had been ugly and hateful between us before he started using drugs became worse with every snort.

He threw hot coffee in my face, giving me third-degree burns. He used my nose as a punching bag so many times that I could taste blood running down my throat when I sang. He broke my jaw. And I couldn't remember what it was like *not* to have a black eye. He thought he was demonstrating his power over me. But the harder he tried to humiliate me and break my spirit, the more important it was for me to be stoic, to pretend that I was unaffected by his abuse, to behave as if I were above it. The people closest to us saw what was happening, but they couldn't stop him. Friends like Rhonda (who also suffered pain and humiliation at his hands, when he did things like pull her hair) knew him well enough to understand that any attempt to help me would make him more violent. Ike was spiraling out of control with alarming speed.

This was in the early 1970s, when domestic abuse was not the issue it is today. I was a frequent visitor to the emergency room, although most of the time I just pulled myself together after a beating and showed up at the next performance, bruises and all. I found that makeup, a big smile, and some flashy dance moves distracted the audience from my wounds. If the doctors thought it was unusual that I came in so often, and had so many "accidents," they didn't say anything. They probably thought that was just the way black people were, fighting like that, especially husbands and wives.

Ike actually sent me to a therapist once. Oh, Ike was a trip. Now that I'm old and I think about it, sometimes I laugh. *He* sent *me* to a therapist. I didn't hold back. I told the therapist about our problems; the singing, our home life, the difficulties of being a single mother, how Ike wasn't a good father. At the end of the session, the therapist said, "I think your husband is the one I need to see." I went back to the studio and told Ike he should make an appointment. That never happened.

I wished he would stay away from me, that he would find someone else, that one of his mistresses would take my place, so I could get out of there. But, behind my back, Ike referred to me as "my million dollars." I didn't fully understand what that meant until later. He was depending on *me* to bring in the money that paid the bills, so he was never going to let me go.

We were one of those families that got all mixed up partly because of the type of marriage it was, built around the musician's life. We'd spend three months on the road, then the next three months working six or seven days a week in places within driving distance of L.A., and Ike considered San Francisco, which was almost four hundred miles away (and parts of Arizona, for that matter), to be within driving distance! After three months at home, we'd go back on the road and the cycle would begin again. There was always a housekeeper to take care of the boys while we were away—Duke's wife, Birdie; Ann Cain, who was one of the "Anns" who became Ike's mistresses; and others. My sister Alline lived nearby and she was a loving aunt who always kept watch on her nephews.

It wasn't a normal household. I tried not to think about how Ike's behavior was affecting our children. I had to be both mother and father to them because Ike was not the kind of man to care about being a good father. "I have neither chicken nor child; when I eat a hamburger, my family is full," he used to say, which was his odd way of expressing that he was not a family man. He was always locked up in the studio, and whenever he did make an appearance at home, he was quick to punish the kids.

I learned how to be a mother by watching the Hendersons, the family I'd worked for back in Tennessee. They showed me how to care for a child, and how important it was to teach them proper behavior. Whenever I was home with the boys, I made sure that we ate our meals together and talked about what was going on in their lives. We did their homework, and I went to see their games. I was happy when Rhonda came into our lives because she was a big help with the kids. She'd pile us into the car and we'd take them on excursions to carnivals and other places where they could have fun.

My boys, who now ranged in age from eleven to thirteen, were growing up, and as they got older, there were moments when my Tina Turner image was a problem for them. They wished their mother could be like the other mothers, and here I was, an R&B, rock 'n' roll singer and dancer, known for being a little raunchy onstage. I tried to make up for that by being very strict and proper at home. I insisted that the boys had to be respectful at all times, and I never allowed them to curse or use slang.

Rules and best intentions aside, children get into trouble: that's

---

what makes them children. But Ike had no patience for that. If one of the boys did something wrong, they all ran to their rooms to hide because they knew he would punish everybody, not just the guilty party. That was his mentality. When the boys got older, I was worried that they would be disturbed by Ike's drug abuse, his infidelities, and the way he treated me. Or that they would find his dangerous, bad boy ways seductive, as any teenager might. They saw the entourage, the parties, the flashy clothes and cars, the ever-present bankroll. I prayed they wouldn't follow Ike's example by using drugs, breaking the law, or acting violent and domineering. But the odds were definitely against them.

In fact, I think Ike was a little bit envious of Craig, who was his stepson. Unlike Ike Jr., Michael, and Ronnie, Craig was diligent in school—did well, graduated—and his behavior was always correct. While Ike would never admit it, he was jealous of the brief relationship I'd had with Craig's father, Raymond.

I never doubted that Ike was suffering. He very seldom had a happy moment, and when he did, we were all so happy that *he* was happy that we almost cheered it, and he would laugh. The rest of the time, he kept trouble around him, like a cloud. He was miserable, no matter how great things were. He had fame, success, a beautiful family, and the possessions he treasured—a fur coat, a diamond watch, the best clothes—the best of the best. But he was just in the dark and never came out of the dark.

And I wasn't the only one he treated badly. To Ike, everyone was the enemy. Even at the airport, he would climb across the counter and threaten to hit the woman selling tickets because she might have said something he didn't like. He was totally out of control, ruled by demons he just couldn't handle or begin to understand.

Forget about whether I was happy, or if the kids were happy, or even if *Ike* was happy. The big loser in this situation was his music. Ike was a hard worker and he had real musical talent, but he didn't advance. He didn't move on. He got stuck in one style of music, one type of singing delivery, the same songs over and over again, sung the same way. He stayed in a groove for days on end, sometimes obsessing so long on a song that it turned into nonsense. He'd play it three or four different ways, with the same melody and pattern. No one in his entourage had the nerve to tell him to stop. They all were too high on cocaine to know better. That's why Ike didn't get on the charts, or get many hit records. In this business, you have to *evolve* to succeed, and Ike didn't know how.

I, on the other hand, was quietly trying to do just that . . . *evolve.* After my suicide attempt, there were two Tinas. There was Ike's Tina, who said and did all the right things. I worked hard onstage. I jumped out of bed in the middle of the night when Ike insisted I race to that hellhole of a studio to record a track that had to be done *that minute,* or else. I fed him soup, massaged his feet, listened to his irrational rants, and took his blows. What was more hurtful than his physical abuse was watching him spend *our* money on women, drugs, and any other indulgences that crossed his mind.

The other Tina had gotten really good at hiding her innermost thoughts. Whatever was happening with Ike, I tried to stay calm, collected, and a little remote. It may sound unlikely, but my role model during these difficult times—and the woman I admired most for her ability to project grace and control in any situation—was Jacqueline Kennedy Onassis.

I admired both Kennedys, the President and the First Lady, when

I first became aware of them in the 1960s. They were the reason I started paying attention to politics. I watched Jackie so closely, studying her every move, and was so impressed by the way she spoke and dressed that I thought, *I want to be like her.* Not exactly like her, but my own version. I remember even wearing pearls. I went out and bought a strand, and everyone was saying, "Oh, Tina Turner is wearing pearls." I don't know if they were making fun of me. But why shouldn't I wear pearls? I put my own twist on the look by pairing them with my funky clothes, and I loved the way it looked.

My appreciation of Jacqueline Kennedy Onassis went beyond loving her incredible sense of style. Beneath her composed façade, she was insecure, uncertain, vulnerable. I read that she was self-conscious about her large hands. She worried about money. She struggled to have a second life after enduring terrible tragedy. I could relate to all of this, and her ability to carry on was a source of hope and inspiration to me.

I met her once, and the moment is still so vivid in my mind that it could have happened yesterday. The Ike and Tina Turner Revue had just performed somewhere, probably in the Boston area, and Ethel Kennedy invited us to come to Hyannis Port to meet her children. We went to the Kennedy compound, where we all danced and had a wonderful time.

Not long after that, Ike and I were checking into a hotel in New York and I saw Jackie and an older woman walking into the lobby from the restaurant. Immediately, I went into a kind of shock. Before I knew what was happening, I dropped my bags and ran straight over to her. Normally, you didn't do that when you were with Ike. You stayed put, like a good dog, right by his side. But this time I couldn't contain myself.

I said, "Uh . . . uh . . . Mrs. Kennedy, I mean Mrs. Onassis, I'm Tina Turner and I just want to say hello."

She looked at me and with that distinctive little voice and said, "Oh, hello." And then she made a tiny gesture with her hand, and of course I caught it and I quickly extended *my* hand.

"You were just in Hyannis Port with Ethel," she said. I was delighted to hear her say that because it meant Ethel had told her about our time together and she already knew a little bit about me.

Jackie was so gracious, but the woman who was with her was looking me up and down with a really negative attitude, willing me to move along. I wanted to say, "If she's being nice to me," meaning Jackie, "then you, whoever you are, should be nice." Then I turned and saw Aristotle Onassis standing there, and I said excitedly, "Oh hi, hello," as if I knew him, too. God, I was a mess. But I was truly overwhelmed to be in her company.

When Ike and I went up to our room, I was still shaking because I was so nervous. I had just met my idol—the woman I revered above all other women. I loved her for her life, her strength, her serenity. And I loved her for the kindness she showed me that day. Even though Ike knew how I felt about Jackie, and what she meant to me, guess what he said? No, I can't tell you. It's too crude. As you can imagine, it was sexual. That's how it was with Ike, and that's why I was always so happy to get away from him.

It may sound silly, but one of my favorite escapes, and a secret pleasure, was driving my Jaguar. I loved it because it was something I could do by myself, one of the few times I could be alone and free. You might be thinking, *Tina, how did you afford a Jaguar?* Well, the great Sammy Davis Jr. bought me my first Jaguar in 1970, after we did a show together in Las Vegas. I remember him as an incredible talent, a true visionary. The first time we worked together on his variety show in the late sixties, he introduced us with an early version of a "rap."

So I don't want to waste a second with idle chatter
We gonna get right down to the meat of the matter
To open up the show tonight we have a treat for you
And I warn you, you will not be able to sit in your seat
'Cause it's Ike and Tina Turner, Ike and Tina Turner,
Ike and Tina Turner, and their revue . . . for you

We had such a good time working with Sammy that we returned to Las Vegas in 1970 to join him on an episode of the popular television show *The Name of the Game.*

Some entertainers express their thanks by sending flowers, but Sammy was a bighearted man who did everything in a big way. He pulled Rhonda aside and whispered that he wanted to surprise me with a car. I think he suggested a Mercedes, but Rhonda, bless her heart, told him that I was into English cars. Presto! Like magic, a gorgeous, white XJ6 Jaguar was waiting for me outside of the hotel. Ike didn't mind because he knew that Sammy wasn't coming on to me: he always treated me like a respected coworker.

Sammy's gift awakened my passion for fast cars. In 1973, Ike decided I should also have the new Jaguar XKE V12 roadster. He sent Rhonda to buy the car and I picked it up. I'll never forget the moment I got behind the wheel and pulled out of the dealership. My life was so controlled that whenever the least bit of light and air came through, it was a big deal. It was late and a little misty when I drove that sleek silver Jaguar on Wilshire Boulevard. As far as I was concerned, there was no one else on the road—just me, driving with the windows down, looking and feeling fabulous. I can still hear the sound of the motor, the *vroom* that signaled it was ready to take me anywhere I wanted to go—that is, if I'd had anywhere to go. I knew I would never drive it at top speed, but I still got the adrenaline rush that car lovers experience. I looked forward to leaving the studio at night because it was always a pleasure to slide into the Jaguar and drive myself to the house. It was only five minutes away, but it was five minutes I could call my own.

I also felt my chains lifting when I started paying attention to matters of the spirit and the soul. I'm a seeker, so I've always been drawn to psychics and readers. I believe there is a higher conscious-ness, and I strive to get to the place where I can truly understand life's meanings and patterns. I want to see my life unfold in fast-forward, like a movie, and a really good psychic can present it that way. Not that they just predict the future (although I always enjoyed that, espe-cially when the prediction was that I would achieve great success on my own!). I find that psychics also help me to think clearly about my choices and actions.

When life with Ike was at its worst, I turned to Buddhism to help me through the bad times. Several people, including my younger son, Ronnie, said that I might benefit from it. Chanting, they suggested, could actually help me to change things in my life. My son said, "Mother, you can get anything you want." That's what he'd heard from his friends. I didn't expect *that* to happen. But I thought maybe this was something that could help me.

I learned a little more about Nichiren Buddhism from one of my friends, and then I started practicing slowly, chanting secretly at first, because I knew Ike wasn't going to like it. I grew up saying the Lord's Prayer, so I was open to the idea of chanting, which is just another form of prayer. I stayed with the Lord's Prayer in the beginning, and then did ten to fifteen minutes of the chant "*Nam-myoho-renge-kyo.*" I wasn't sure what the words meant because the literature didn't really explain it, but as I stumbled through the little book on Buddhism my friend had given me, I learned not to worry so much about what I was saying. All I needed to know was that the sound was touching a part of me, deep inside, putting me in another frame of mind.

Chanting, I discovered, removed uncomfortable attitudes from my thoughts. I started to think differently. Everything became lighter. I needed a new mind-set to deal with my horrible marriage, and my "practice," as it's called, was helping me to reprogram my brain, to move into the light, to make the right decisions. The more I did it, the stronger I felt.

Someone once asked me about the relationship between singing and chanting. I explained that chanting is not necessarily like singing a song, rather it's that moment when you find yourself making sounds from within—from your heart, from your spirit. Each person has a song inside. That is something I learned over time. You can find the hum inside of you that can give you peace when you are really down. Mama Georgie, my grandmother, had a hum, never a song. She would sit in a rocking chair and just hum, and I would listen. There was no real melody, but I know now that it was her way of touching a place deep inside her. It was the song of her soul. Everyone should try to find the song within.

I wish more people could understand how important meditation and prayer are—how important it is to be spiritual. When I say "spiritual," well, that can scare people—they think religion, church, God—but being spiritual means touching the highest part of yourself. I went from my Baptist prayers to Buddhism—different words at a time when I needed different words—but I was always spiritual. My practice helps me to not be upset: to deal with situations on a different level because I think about them differently.

I still get upset occasionally, I'm only human. But chanting always makes me feel better. When I embraced Buddhism, I realized that I, alone, was responsible for my life, and what I wanted it to be.

If I had any doubts about the power of Buddhism, they evaporated the moment Ike reacted so negatively to my chanting. He came across my *butsudan*, a little cabinet that held candles, incense, water, fruit, and other traditional essentials for my practice, which I had hidden in an empty room. "Get that motherfucker out of my house," he ordered. Profanity aside, I could tell that it made him uneasy to think I had a secret life, and a mysterious one at that. As far as he was concerned, Buddhism was a form of voodoo, and he didn't like it, or trust it. Typically, he was afraid of anything he didn't understand. I liked having a little power over him for a change. I could see that he was the fearful one, scared that I would cast a spell on him, or something silly like that.

I decided that maybe my chanting was working after all, when, in 1974, I was offered the role of the Acid Queen in Ken Russell's film of the Who's rock opera *Tommy*. Ike kept me on a very short leash, so it was exciting whenever there was an opportunity to get out from under his shadow. I was thrilled. Acting had been one of my ambitions when I was a child. I'd come home from seeing a movie and recreate the most dramatic scenes for any family member who had the patience to watch. I especially loved doing really over-the-top death scenes.

———

I headed to London, where the film was being shot, certain I was on my way to becoming a movie star. I took great pride in the way I dressed, so I brought my own clothes to the set, just in case I didn't like the costumes. Thank God! You should have seen how they would have dressed me. I pleaded, "Please. I brought my own Yves Saint Laurent skirt and accessories." The costume designer, Russell's wife, Shirley, said that I could wear them, although she came up with the Acid Queen's clunky platform shoes. Ken Russell loved the way I looked. I do remember him saying he hadn't known I had so much hair, but it worked for the character.

It was one of those rare trips that Ike let me take alone (he was busy with something in L.A.), and the whole time I was in London, I felt like a bird who had escaped from a cage. I was so happy that Ike wasn't involved in any way—that there wasn't one guitar for him to play, and I said to myself, "I can do this without you." I wasn't allowed to *say* that, of course. But the fact that Ike knew there was a demand for me without him—for the second time, counting my experience with Phil Spector on "River Deep—Mountain High"—was really satisfying.

It sounds crazy to say now, but at the time, I had no idea that the Acid Queen had any connection to drugs. So much for my wild and crazy life! Still, I felt perfectly comfortable playing this wild lady in *Tommy*. Why shouldn't I? By this point, I'd been singing professionally for sixteen years, and performing onstage *is* a form of acting: in both worlds, great care goes into creating a look, projecting an attitude, interpreting the words, *performing*—in my case, the lyrics of a song. I loved doing the film and hoped there'd be more opportunities to act in the future.

While I was in London, my friend Ann-Margret, who was starring in *Tommy*, invited me to appear on her television special, *Ann-Margret Olsson*. I first met Ann-Margret in 1973, when Ike and I were performing at the International Hotel in Las Vegas and she was at the Tropicana. Rhonda and I slipped out from Ike's watchful eye to catch her act and visited her dressing room after the show. When her husband, Roger Smith, opened the door, he was shocked to see me standing there. "You're not going to believe this," he said, "but Ann-Margret is a huge fan of yours and has all of your albums." Then he showed me a stack of them right there!

We became good friends after that night and had a great time working together on skits and songs for the television show, including a spirited delivery of "Nutbush City Limits," the hit song I'd written about my hometown. The words "A church house, gin house" came naturally to me—these were my childhood memories set to music. I actually got paid royalties when the song became a hit—which was incredible to me because I *still* didn't get paid for anything else at the time. That check was one more taste of independence.

Now that I was spending more and more time outside the bubble, I think Ike sensed that he was losing his hold on me. Whether I was chanting or working on a job that didn't include him, I was distancing myself from "Ike and Tina."

A partner of yours will fall, like a leaf from a tree in autumn, the psychic had predicted all those years ago.

The spell was lifting, a door was opening, and I was taking baby steps away from Ike. *A change is gonna come* . . .

Those baby steps turned into a giant leap in July 1976, when we flew into Dallas for a show. During previous trips to Dallas we had performed sold-out shows at Lovall's and at the Skyliner in Fort Worth, so we were looking forward to coming back. But the plane ride that day was uncomfortable because Ike was recovering from one of his five-day cocaine benders and was in a horrible mood. He insisted on draping himself over me and Ann Thomas during the flight. It was humiliating to be with him when he was hung over; I felt that everyone was staring at us.

It got worse when we landed. The weather was hot and uncomfortable—the temperature was in the nineties—and Ike insisted on pulling out a melted chocolate bar to eat in the car. He tried to give me some and I recoiled because I was wearing a white Yves Saint Laurent pantsuit and didn't want to get it dirty. Apparently, my refusal to share his candy was a signal that it was time to fight.

First, we had words. Everything that came out of his mouth was always a profanity. But this time, when he said, "Fuck you," I said, "Fuck you" back. It was as if a voice that had been hiding deep inside me came out for the first time. That was a surprise to Ike, who turned to one of his musicians and said, "Man, this woman never talked to me like that."

Then he started punching me, and reached for his shoe to do the dirty work.

I *really* shocked him. When a lick came, I gave him a lick back, blow for blow. It felt really good to fight this person who had been so rude, vulgar, and abusive for so long. It came to a point where I freaked; it was the last drop that spilled the water out of the bucket. We fought all the way to the Statler Hilton.

By the time we reached the hotel, my face was swollen and my once-beautiful suit was splattered with blood. We attracted a lot of attention when we stepped out of the car, although Ike claimed we had been in an "accident." I looked like a woman who had been broken and silenced. And that's what Ike wanted to believe, that he'd won the round, like he had won all those other fights. The truth was another story.

In our room, I pretended to be the same old Tina: the wife who was understanding and forgiving; the one who was concerned about Ike's needs—his headache, his bloody nose, his exhaustion, his pain. I went through the motions of preparing him for our first show that night: ordering his dinner, massaging his temples, and urging him to take a little nap. He heard what he wanted to hear, but the whole time, I was thinking, *What would happen if I just grabbed a bag and ran?*

Well, that's exactly what I did. As soon as Ike fell asleep, I reached for a small toiletries case, tied a scarf around my throbbing head, and tossed a cape around my shoulders. Then I got the hell out of that room and out of that life.

I might have forgotten it for a while, but I knew how to run away from snakes.

On an adrenaline high, I raced to the first floor, terrified that I would meet one of Ike's entourage, and slipped through the hotel kitchen into an alley. It was dark outside and the landscape was unfamiliar, so I hid among the garbage cans while I figured out what to do next. Unfortunately, the streets behind the hotel did not offer the best cover for a nervous fugitive. The buildings were low and surrounded by open spaces that were filled with weeds. You know what I think? I think that my will to live was so strong that I was blind to danger, because I'm certain that those weeds, which were as high as my waist in some spots, must have been crawling with animals I couldn't see.

I decided to keep moving, afraid that Ike would wake up and catch me, as he had done so many times before. I didn't stop for several blocks, until I came to Interstate 30, where I spotted a Ramada Inn on the other side. There was probably a safer way to get over the busy highway, but I didn't know the area. In my confusion, the most direct route seemed to be running down an embankment and across several lanes of speeding traffic.

As I took my first step, I knew that if I survived, I would be adding *this* story to the list of times I escaped death. I'm not sure what was more frightening—the whooshing sounds the trucks made as they came speeding toward me or the thunderous vibrations I felt with my entire body as they passed. One truck driver blasted his horn at the unlikely sight of a frightened woman running past him on a multilane highway. That's when I realized, you can't compare the speed of the foot to the speed of a ten-wheeler. By the time I reached the middle of the road, the truck was almost on top of me. I just missed getting hit by one of the really big ones, and I'll never know how I escaped death at that moment.

A country girl knows how to run through fields and do all that daredevil stuff. But I felt that I was being guided by a higher power that night. Somehow, I made it across the highway and up the hill to the Ramada, only to realize that there were greater obstacles ahead. Ike always threatened, "When you leave, you leave like you came," meaning with nothing. He was right. I had 36 cents and a Mobil credit card in my pocket, my face was battered, and my clothes were filthy and stained with blood. And I was black. In Dallas. It occurred to me that, under the circumstances, any sensible innkeeper would probably turn me away.

———

I walked up to the desk and introduced myself to the manager, explaining who I was and that I had run away from my husband and didn't have any money. But I swore I would pay him back if he'd give me a room for the night. It crossed my mind that, in my vulnerable condition, this stranger could take advantage of me—even rape me. I was too weary and numb to be afraid, or even care. Lucky for me, the manager had a big heart. He immediately took me upstairs to a suite and promised to send up hot soup and crackers.

When I closed the door, the thought of what I had done hit me so hard that I became weak in the knees, almost faint. My heart was in my ears.

I was terrified, but I was also excited.

I wasn't just running away from Ike. I was running toward a new life.

———

6

"WHEN THE HEARTACHE IS OVER"

" Time to move on
with my life now

Leaving the past
all behind **"**

I f I told you that I woke up in a panic the day after my escape—
that I doubted I would be able to figure out how to live, how to
support my kids, how to survive Ike's wrath, how to go on—I
would be lying. I may not have had all (or any!) of the answers, but life,
I have to say, was *great* after I left Ike. Even though I had no money
and I knew the kids and I would struggle, the fact that I was out of that
hell meant everything to me. I tasted true freedom for the first time
in fourteen years. I was nervous—that was natural—but I was also
curious to see how I would get along on my own. At the age of thirty-
seven, I was starting over.

Of course, I had to start dealing with practical matters the moment I returned to Los Angeles. Ike's accountant, who was very kind
to me, had arranged for an airline ticket from Dallas to L.A. I decided
to leave the kids with Ike at the house for the time being. I call them
"kids," but they were well into their teens at the time. My son Craig
was almost as old as I was when I gave birth to him, and he had a
steady girlfriend, Bernadette. I knew that my sister, my mother, and
Ike's housekeeper would take care of the boys while I stayed out of
sight and came up with a strategy.

I had to depend on friends for a place to live, but I couldn't stay
with anyone who knew Ike, or he might find me and try to force me
to come back. I decided it was safe to get help from my Buddhist
friends, and their friends and relatives. They were kind people who

opened their homes to me, but their lifestyles were a little casual. For two months, I moved from place to place, sometimes living in a spare room, other times carving out a corner for myself in an already cramped space.

Thanks to the time I spent living with the Hendersons when I was young, I was a pretty finicky housekeeper. To this day, I have very high standards. When I found myself in these, let's say, "bohemian" surroundings, my first impulse was to clean and keep cleaning. While my hosts were out, or at work, I scrubbed their homes from top to bottom, organized their closets, and got rid of their junk and trash. A visit from Tina meant that everything would be neat and sparkling. It was my way of creating order out of chaos, *and* of earning my keep. I may not have had any money, but I was rich in elbow grease, and I was happy to be useful. Better to be someone else's maid than Ike Turner's wife was my attitude.

Cleaning was one form of therapy: chanting was another. Followers of Buddhism believe that all things are possible. During this difficult time, I sought the company of my chanting friends because it was so important for me to be among positive people. I knew they would help *me* feel positive. "*Nam-myoho-renge-kyo*," I repeated, sometimes for hour upon hour. With practice, chanting became second nature to me, and I saw that it was really working. I felt a door opening inside me, connecting me to my subconscious mind. My reactions were clear and focused thanks to my practice; I knew because my normal reactions weren't that way. I needed to have my wits about me at all times, and chanting helped me with that. Convincing Ike that I was really and truly gone, and doing it in a way that wouldn't get me killed, was going to be my biggest challenge.

They say there are five stages of grief—denial, anger, bargaining, depression, and acceptance. When Ike woke up from his nap in Dallas and realized I was nowhere to be found (and that there would be no show that night, or in the foreseeable future), he bounced between denial and anger, with a little opportunistic bargaining thrown in. He probably thought that I was just being dramatic by disappearing after our big blowout fight. In his narcissistic mind, he wanted to believe that Tina would be lost without Ike. He locked himself in the studio, turned to his best friend cocaine (and a girlfriend or two) for comfort, and waited for me to come crawling back with my tail between my legs. He told the boys that he was already thinking about going South to find another "Tina," the same way he found the first one. In his mind, it was that easy to replace me.

When I didn't come to him, he came to me. Somehow, Ike figured out I was staying at my friend Anna Maria Shorter's house, and he showed up one day with a bunch of stooges. I called the police, who shooed them away. His next attempt was a little more civil: he actually requested a meeting. I said yes, but going into it, I made up my mind that I didn't care if he beat me, or even tried to kill me. No matter what he said or did, I was never going back.

My strategy was to look as unattractive as possible. I put on too much makeup, which was never my style, and deliberately wore an unflattering dress. Ike pulled up in the Rolls. Duke was the driver that night, just as he had been when we eloped to Tijuana, so I guess we had come full circle. I got into the back with Ike and spoke politely, although I felt anything but polite. I was always nice to him because I knew the rules: don't say *anything* that might trigger a fight.

When we got to the restaurant, we were both visibly uncomfortable. Ike seemed nervous, like he wanted to talk, but didn't know how to approach me. I could have told him what he *should* have said: "My life is ruined," or "I'll really try to do better if you come back," something to convince me that he wanted to change. But those words didn't come naturally to him, and even if he had said all the right things, it wouldn't have worked because I knew how he was, how he would always be.

Right after our meeting, Ike tried another tactic. He packed up all four boys and sent them to me, with enough money for the first month's rent on a house—that was it. I saw his gesture as a dare, as if he was saying, "Go ahead, try to make it out there on your own. I'll see you soon enough, begging for your old life." I reminded myself that I was the girl who liked to take risks. This was a big one, but after I'd stepped out of Ike's world, and had a taste of independence, there was no way I was getting back under his thumb. I just needed a plan.

I called Rhonda, knowing that she could fix *anything* . . . a broken speaker, a car, a life. We always came through for each other, despite Ike's attempts to divide us. The petty jealousies of the past seemed unimportant. We shared a lot of history, some painful, but it was time to think about the future. I asked her to be my manager.

I explained that the wolf was literally at the door. Rhonda was well aware of my legal situation. When I left the Ike and Tina Turner Revue, all of our upcoming concert dates had to be canceled. Since I was the one who dropped out (Ike was willing and able to perform, but there couldn't be a show without me), I was the one getting subpoenaed by the scorched venues for lost revenue. But there was no money. Period. I had to find a way to pay the creditors and support my family, while Ike watched from the comfort of our house and former lifestyle, hoping I would fail.

In her typical no-nonsense, get-the-job-done style, Rhonda swung into action. At the beginning, she found that nobody wanted to take a chance on Tina without Ike. "That's only half of the show," they told her. "It's not going to draw people." We had a very hard time. Since we didn't have any prospects (or a band, or backup singers, or costumes, for that matter), the easiest job to look for was an appearance on a television show. Calling herself "Shannon" so that Ike wouldn't know what she was up to, Rhonda reached out to popular shows like *Hollywood Squares*, *The Brady Bunch*, and *Donnie and Marie*, to offer my services. She'd call and say that I'd *love* to do the show (whatever show it was, I loved it if I could get a booking), and that I was available on such and such a date.

Happily, she was able to schedule an appearance on Cher's top-rated solo variety show. Ike and I had been on it back in 1975, right after she and Sonny divorced, and I think Cher and I surprised each other the first time we met. Expecting the sexy "Tina" she'd seen on-stage, the wild woman who was all legs, fringe, and shimmy, she was unprepared to see that Tina Turner was actually a *lady*, a polished woman who wore a silk shirt, trousers, and high heels, and who never used salty language. Meanwhile, meeting Cher was an eye-opening experience for *me* because I could see how happy she was on her own. Without Sonny, Cher was free. She controlled her career and her private life—her music, her friends, how she spent her time—and that's what I desperately wanted for myself: a world without Ike.

Looking back, I see that there were many similarities in our situations. We were both very young when we met our husbands. Cher was only sixteen when she got together with Sonny. We didn't know how to do the simplest things because we never had to take care of ourselves. Here we were, famous headliners pulling in a lot of money, yet neither one of us knew how to write a check. Many women in the 1960s and 1970s relied on their husbands to take care of the business of life, but we were in the funny position of making all the money without having any control over our income.

Not surprisingly, after we ended our marriages, we both found ourselves embroiled in ugly financial situations that did not work to our advantage. After Cher pulled out of their joint contracts, she owed Sonny two million dollars to make up for lost revenue. My situation was a little different—I got bombarded with lawsuits because of the Ike and Tina cancellations. But Cher and I each determined to do whatever was necessary to win financial independence. Cher says she took on her first gig at Caesars Palace to pay off her debt to Sonny, while I took whatever jobs I could get—no matter how small—until I paid my way out of the whole thing. As long as I was healthy and happy, money wasn't as important to me as my freedom.

Working with Cher was so much fun. We had a wonderful rapport onstage. Whenever I was scheduled for the show, she used to joke about having to get ready for "Hurricane Tina." Cher'd say, "Oh no, I have to exercise because Tina's coming." She knew that I never pitty-patted around when dancing was involved. I always gave my all, and I made her work extra hard to keep up with me, but in a fun way. I think the audience could tell that we enjoyed each other: the affection between us was real.

Appearing on *Hollywood Squares* was another story. It was a popular quiz show with a tic-tac-toe format that featured celebrities sitting in boxes. The celebrities would answer questions, and the contestants had to decide if their answers were right or wrong. The routine was that the producers came into the dressing room beforehand to preview the topics, and I remember being proud of myself for being knowledgeable. I felt pretty comfortable, until the show started and host Peter Marshall said to me, "Tina . . . where's Ike?"—which was the *last* thing I wanted to hear. I found it a bit unnerving. Then the questions, which I was hearing for the first time, started. I discovered that when we were on the air, the topics were a *little* different from what we'd discussed, so it was unlikely you'd answer correctly. I got a few right, but I did stumble, and that bothered me even though I knew it was part of the game. Well, when my episode of *Squares* came on, my boys couldn't stop making fun of me. "Mother's on a television show, making an ass of herself," they joked when they thought I couldn't hear them. I tried to defend myself, but they wouldn't listen.

No matter. I had to swallow my pride and do a lot of things to keep us afloat. I always tried to maintain my sense of humor. I called those days "Tina's Operation Oops," because there were so many "oops" when I was first figuring out how to be on my own. At a certain point, I released myself from the burden of getting everything right. I realized that I didn't have to be intimidated by not knowing, or hide my inexperience. I could simply say, "No, I don't know that," and promise myself that I would learn from my mistakes and do better next time. My only goal was to survive.

I found us a little house on Sunset Crest in Laurel Canyon and rented everything, from furniture to dishes, to make a proper home for my boys. I still didn't allow slang in the house, and I still cared a lot about their manners. But I had more pressing concerns. I didn't want the boys to be spoiled brats, so this was the moment to teach them to be more independent. It was a hard battle because they were used to having maids and nannies—there was always someone to pick up after them, especially when we were on the road. Now they resented the fact that their circumstances had changed, especially when they saw Ike enjoying the same self-indulgent lifestyle as before. But I think it was a good lesson for them to learn.

I wasn't depressed by our reduced circumstances. It's my nature to be optimistic. Anytime there's a separation or divorce, there's a change, with possibilities for a whole new life, in whatever direction you take it. When you have nothing, you're starting fresh, I told myself, and I liked that. Rhonda and I got really good at turning a dime into a dollar. I'd make a little money for doing an appearance, then Rhonda and I would go over the basic expenses that had to be paid—rent, gas, food (I actually signed up for food stamps to help with the groceries), and lawsuits. By the time we finished paying the bills, there'd be about ten dollars left, and we'd split it! We were the original "Two Broke Girls," and we weren't above using Blue Chip Stamps (the California version of Green Stamps) to get the household items we needed. Luckily, Rhonda had a few credit cards for emergencies, and believe me, we put them to good use, more often than we should have.

I filed for divorce pretty quickly because I wanted to settle things with Ike once and for all. But he took every opportunity to stall. He was in denial, still believing that Ike and Tina would get back together, at least as performers. I set him straight at a meeting with Mike Stewart. Mike was the head of United Artists, our most recent record label. Speaking for Ike, he asked if I would be willing to go back. Ike would give me everything he knew I wanted, Mike promised.

I told him, "No, Mike. I know how *that* is. I can't go back to that environment because it's dangerous. Ike will forget all about this meeting as soon as he's in the studio doing cocaine." At that point, I thought Ike might jump over the table to fight with me. I didn't know what I would do next, or how I would support myself, but I refused to be intimidated. There would be no new record contract and no collaboration of any kind, professional or personal, with Ike Turner. We were finished.

For some reason, Ike was surprised. To him, my refusal was like pouring gasoline on a fire—he saw red. Once he understood that I was gone, he struck back the only way he knew how, with violence. He wanted to punish me, and Rhonda, too, once he found out about her disloyalty. The scary thing was he had foot soldiers who were willing to do whatever he asked. Ike always surrounded himself with goons who liked to think of themselves as outlaws. Preying on two single women and four teenagers was about as cowardly as a "gangster" could get, but that's exactly what they did.

One night we were at home and we heard this loud *bang, bang, bang* coming from outside. When we looked, we saw that the back window of Rhonda's car had been blown out with bullets. Another night, they actually shot into the house. We were so scared that Rhonda slept on the floor of the boys' room and I slept in my closet because the room had a skylight and I was afraid there might be more shooting. Later, a friend of Rhonda's heard that Ike's goons were bragging about what they did. Then there was the time someone started a fire around Craig's girlfriend's car, which was parked in front of the house. We had to run for water and blankets to put it out.

It was important for me to think clearly during this terrifying time. I started chanting four hours a day—two hours in the morning and two in the evening—to help me focus. I also took some, shall we say, "practical" steps to protect myself after I heard from a reliable source that Ike was talking to someone about solving his Tina problem. He tried to arrange for a hit man to "take me to the ballpark," or the "football field," or whatever the expression is. That was enough to convince me to ask a friend to help me get a gun, and once I had it, I kept it close at all times. Ike made a point of sending people I didn't know to do his dirty work, so I was always wary of strangers, paranoid that they were following me.

One day, while I was out driving, I was stopped by the police. They saw something in my car that made them want to ask me a few questions. At their request, I got out of the car and stepped over to the curb. When they asked where I was going, I explained that I was on my way to a chanting meeting, which was absolutely true. The officer looked a little puzzled and said, "Then why do you have a gun?" *That's* why they'd pulled me over—because they saw the gun, in plain sight, sticking out of my purse. The gun that was supposed to save me from Ike. I hadn't realized it was so visible, or the dangers of driving around with it on display in a Jaguar.

Buddhism and a firearm must have seemed like a *really* strange combination. Trying to defend myself, I started talking about my husband, Ike Turner, and how I didn't feel safe because he was going to take me to the "ballpark." They knew all about Ike at the station—it seems that everyone knew about Ike —but they warned me that having a husband who wants to kill you is no excuse to carry a loaded weapon in a vehicle, which was against the law in California. Lesson learned.

There were times when I felt so alone. Muh sided with Ike, if you can believe it. In her mind, he was always right because he had the big house, the Cadillac, the money. And, if you asked her, she definitely thought that he had all the talent. "You need him," she told me repeatedly, refusing to see that I had my own talent. I tried to explain to her that she didn't understand what it was like living with Ike—that I would never go back. No matter what I said, Muh favored Ike and stayed close to him, almost as if she was *his* mother. That hurt, but it wasn't a surprise after so many years of being invisible to her.

But I didn't have time to lick old wounds. I had to work, and fortunately, I was able to convince Mike Stewart to give me an advance to underwrite a proper act. Rhonda booked us in cabaret settings at hotels and casinos, venues that skewed a little older and tamer than I was used to, but I was thrilled to be back onstage with musicians and dancers, selecting my own material, my own costumes (courtesy of famed designer Bob Mackie, whom I met when I worked with Cher), and my own schedule. I was independent for the very first time.

I tried to hold on to that feeling, the excitement and optimism that propelled me every time I walked out onstage. And the truth is, it didn't matter if five people came, or five hundred, I always believed that the audience was entitled to the same wonderful show, with me at my absolute best. I didn't care that there were wardrobe malfunctions (we didn't call them that then, but there was the night when I went one way and my "Big Spender" costume went the other!), or that I was sued at every job—the process servers showed up with their hands out as soon as they heard Tina Turner was performing.

Being on the road was hard, but coming home was difficult, too. When I traveled, I always made arrangements for the boys to have some kind of help from a housekeeper or my mother and Alline, who would deliver meals to them. I say "boys" by habit: Craig, Ike Jr., Michael, and Ronnie were young men. One time I came home when they weren't expecting me and walked into a cartoon version of a bachelor pad. An unimaginable mess! I could barely get up the stairs, there was so much stuff all over the place. "Uh-oh, here's Mother," they complained to each other when I surprised them. They were big enough to know better and I let them have it.

Another time, I came home from a tour to an empty house. It was Christmas. I don't remember where the boys were, but I was all alone. I lit the fireplace (I've loved fireplaces since I was a child), sat in the living room, and that was my holiday. There was one lone gift under the tree, a vase from my law firm (I still have it). I remember thinking it held the prettiest flowers I had ever seen, probably because it was my only Christmas present. But it was okay. Every time I found myself in this kind of situation, I always accepted it. Instead of being depressed, I reminded myself that I was home and could take this opportunity to enjoy the quiet. It was my nature to be happy.

The longer I was away from Ike, the less patience I had for the dark clouds in his troubled world. He was still stalking me and often surfaced when I least expected him. One night, he and two of his goons came to the airport when I was flying out for a show. Ike tried to act tough with my musicians and the young man I had hired to be our guard—I traveled with security because I never knew what might happen. The musicians looked at Ike as if to say, "Don't even think about causing trouble." They wanted to get on that flight and go to work, and it made me feel good that they were supportive.

Then Ike stared at the security guard, who didn't know him, and said, "Who the fuck are you?" I *never* spoke that way, and I felt terrible for the guard. The poor guy thought his job was to deal with overly enthusiastic fans, not a crazy, foulmouthed husband. Ike added insult to injury by calling him a "sausage ass." The guard was a little portly, but he'd never heard *that* insult before. What Ike didn't realize was that the "sausage ass" was connected to the Los Angeles mafia. I didn't even know there was such a thing, but the next day, I got a call from a nice older man who said he knew all about what happened at the airport and asked if I needed "help" handling Ike. I guess they were offering to take him to the "ballpark." I was so flustered that I made some appreciative noises and handed the phone to Rhonda.

It sounds a little bit like a comedy, but these incidents were frightening at the time because they really were life-threatening. You never knew if Ike and his thugs were carrying guns or knives, and we really didn't know what they were capable of doing. I think that's when I truly realized our situation was not normal. Marriages dissolve all the time without the help of weapons and hit men. It was time to accelerate the divorce.

There was so much haggling over assets that the process was taking forever. The day that we went to the judge's chamber to finalize the terms of the divorce, Ike was giving me threatening looks. I wanted to say, "You're such an idiot. Do you think your vibes can even reach me now? You have no power over me." The judge said to me, "Young lady, what do you want?" When I mentioned that I'd left some jewelry at the studio, Ike snapped, "There's no jewelry."

I saw where this was going. Ike planned on using the divorce to keep us tied to each other. It would have been constant war, with more and more arguing, and there was only one way to end it. I told the judge, "Forget the jewelry. Forget everything. It's only blood money. I want nothing." He asked if I was sure. I said I was very sure although

I did have *one* request. I wanted to continue using the name "Tina Turner," which Ike owned because of the trademark he had obtained when we first started performing as the Ike and Tina Turner Revue. The judge ruled in my favor, and I walked out of that courtroom with the name Tina Turner and my two Jaguars, the one from Sammy Davis Jr. and the one from Ike, and that's it.

It seems so funny now—no money for food, rent, or other necessities, no idea of how to pay the bills, but two Jaguars! I knew what Ike was thinking. That woman's too old. She's not going to do anything. Denial, denial, denial. Considering my age, thirty-nine, my gender, my color, and the times we lived in, everything was strong winds against me. And you know what I say to people who ask, "What do you do when all the odds are against you?" I say, "You keep going. You just don't stop. No matter, if there's one slap to the face, turn the other cheek. And the hurt you're feeling? You can't think about what's being done to you now, or what has been done to you in the past. You just have to keep going."

7

"OVERNIGHT SENSATION"

" Two dollar high-heel shoes and a honky tonk dress

In the rhythm and the soul reviews I had a dream I guess "

S o that's what I did. I just kept going. I never said, "Well, I don't have this and I don't have that." I said, "I don't have this *yet*, but I'm going to get it." The way I was thinking, I was choreographing my own life, figuring out which steps to take and, more importantly, picking the right time to take them.

I remember one day when I was lying in bed, feeling a little overwhelmed, and saying to myself, "I have to get management." It was 1979. Rhonda was doing a good job booking me on the cabaret circuit, but I had dreams, and they were big. I wanted to fill concert halls and arenas, like the Rolling Stones and Rod Stewart. That was quite an ambition for a forty-year-old female singer whose best years seemed to be behind her. Then again, I never thought about age. I didn't look forty. I was wearing wigs, so if I was gray underneath, no one could see it! I was still dancing, running across the stage in fact. I felt young and energetic. What I needed was a professional to help me get my career on the right track.

Rava Daly, one of my dancers, kept talking about a manager she knew named Lee Kramer, whose client at the time was Olivia Newton-John. Rava urged me to talk to Lee and his associate, an Australian named Roger Davies, who had just come to America. I listened to her and made an appointment to see them. Roger knew all about Ike and Tina, and he was familiar with my song "Nutbush City Limits" because it had been a big hit in Australia. He was a young man, only twenty-six, but he had quite the background in music. Before Roger moved to America, he'd worked as a musician and a roadie, and he managed the popular Australian group Sherbet during their most successful years.

Today, Roger and I joke about that fateful meeting and our funny first impressions of each other. I thought that Roger looked much older than he was, more like he was in his early forties. And I never saw anyone buried in so much *stuff*—his office was bursting with books, records, everything—all piled around him as if he was a hoarder.

What did he think of me? Given my long-standing history with Ike, Roger expected me to look much older. The wig always made me appear younger than my years, and my clothes were youthful. He listened to a mix of my music, didn't seem all that impressed, and looked at me as if he wasn't sure he knew what to do with this odd bundle of contradictions. Roger didn't talk much, but when he did, he chose his words carefully. "What do you want?" he asked thoughtfully.

I was brutally honest because there was no point in being otherwise. One thing I had learned about myself since I left Ike and went out on my own was that I was ambitious. I said, "Well, I just got a divorce. I'm in debt. I need a manager. I need a record company. I need records. And [by the way] I want to fill halls like the Rolling Stones and Rod Stewart." There, I put all my cards on the table. If Roger thought my answer was crazy, he didn't say so. I told him I was playing the Venetian Room at the Fairmont Hotel in San Francisco and invited him to fly up with Lee Kramer to see my act.

I felt so much better when I left his office because I had actually done something about the future. I didn't know whether or not he would make it to the show—just because he said he'd come didn't mean he would—but by reaching out to him, I'd taken a step in the right direction. I was taking control of my career in an informed way, making moves and choices, and that was empowering and exciting.

In San Francisco, the Fairmont audience was sweet, but a little stuffy. The regulars at the Venetian Room were more of a fancy night-club crowd than the fans who usually came to see the Ike and Tina Turner Revue. They dressed to the nines and sat comfortably at tables while they drank cocktails and watched the show. My act was still evolving, but it had to showcase my talents in a cabaret setting, which was different from the places I'd played with Ike. My costumes were a combination of old things I'd worn before and some gorgeous new designs by Bob Mackie, with lots of skin, sparkle, and glitz. To make the music timely, I blended popular hits like "Disco Inferno" with old favorites like "Proud Mary."

Whenever I looked out at the crowd, I hoped to see Roger and Lee, but they kept me waiting for two weeks. They didn't make it to San Francisco until the very last night of the show. When I saw these two young guys in the room—I still get emotional when I think about it—it was so meaningful to me. I thought, *They came . . . great!* I knew I had a good show because I was *free.* Finally, I was dancing on my own. I had my own band playing what I wanted them to play, at the tempo I wanted. I never did it for the money. I did it for love of the work, and the audience felt that emotion coming from the stage. It lifted them. The ladies in their black dresses and pearls stood up and moved with the music. I'll never forget the headline in one of the San Francisco newspapers. It said something like, "Tina Turner Pulled Cobwebs Out of Nob Hill Last Night." And it was true!

Roger and Lee came backstage after the show. Lee was appreciative, but Roger was *really* enthusiastic, which pleased me enormously because I could tell that he was the hungry one, the one who would do the work. It was our destiny to come together at this moment, two people standing on the brink of new lives. He wanted an artist. I wanted a manager. His ambition was to build a star, and I needed someone to believe in me, to take me to that place. We both got what we wanted. I think Roger is the brother I never had, and I'm the sister he never had. We bonded the moment we started working together.

Rhonda understood that I needed a manager with a long-term plan. Roger was good at everything, but what really impressed me about him was that he recognized the importance of building an audience in Europe. A lot of Americans in the music business didn't acknowledge that the rest of the world existed. Roger, probably because he was foreign, always thought globally. He had me working internationally, everywhere from Poland to Asia. And with his help, I stripped my act of the Las Vegas/nightclub elements, the flashy costumes and set pieces. We streamlined the dancers and dressed the band in black karate suits. The musicians hated them, but they were inexpensive and they didn't stand out. Just as I'd imagined, we were making the show more rock 'n' roll. I was the happiest I'd ever been, happier than I'd ever dreamed I could be.

The most challenging part was finding a record company. I remember Roger saying, "Darling"—he always called me "Darling"—"Every door I walk through, I say 'Tina,' they say, 'Ike.'" Record executives in America were brainwashed about Ike, who had a terrible reputation for being dangerous and unpredictable. Now his bad behavior was tainting me. Roger had never imagined it would be so hard to get a label, but he never gave up. Instead, he thought strategically, which is what made him a wonderful manager. He knew that there were many routes to a record contract. He was trying to figure out which one was right for me. I think he was always amazed by my certainty that everything would work out.

"Don't worry, Roger, we'll be fine," I told him over and over again.

Roger was also managing Olivia Newton-John at the time. It really says something about the breadth of his talent as a manager that he was able to guide two artists who were so different from each other. One day, he came to me with a song that he loved and urged me to record it. I had to be honest with him—I always was—and I said I couldn't imagine myself singing that song, so I passed on it. He brought the song to Olivia. It was "Physical," which was absolutely perfect for her, and it sold millions of copies and became her biggest hit. I knew that *my* song was out there, somewhere. We just had to find it.

My Cinderella moment happened in New York's East Village, at a club called the Ritz. Roger wanted me to perform at a space where I could really connect with the audience, and the Ritz was a wonderful old concert hall that attracted real downtown music lovers. I appeared there twice in 1981, and on one of those nights Rod Stewart was in the house. When he heard me sing his hit song "Hot Legs," he asked me to perform it with him on *Saturday Night Live*, where he was going to be the musical guest. "We've got a surprise for you," he told the NBC audience, saying that it gave him pleasure to introduce "someone who has been a great inspiration to me" (prompting one band member to quip, "Doris Day?"). Rod dismissed that idea and called me onto the stage. We had such a good time bringing the song to life. I high-kicked my heart out every time we said the word "legs." It was a wonderful opportunity for me to reach a new audience—all those young *Saturday Night Live* fans who may not have known my work and were seeing me at my "Hot Legs" best. It was the beginning of great times for me.

After another night at the Ritz, I received a surprise invitation from the Rolling Stones, who asked me to open some of their concerts during their North American tour. Singing "Honky Tonk Woman" with the band at the Brendan Byrne Arena in the New Jersey Meadowlands, one of the giant venues of my dreams, was everything I'd hoped it would be. That crowd! The experience was quite a contrast to my intimate cabaret appearances.

During my third appearance at the Ritz, in 1983, the stars aligned, literally and figuratively, in a way I had never imagined possible. I had this thing with Roger. I asked him not to tell me when there were celebrities in the audience—none of that "guess who's here tonight"— because I would find it distracting. I was there to entertain my fans and, in my mind, *everyone* in the audience was a VIP.

Apparently, a lot happened before I sang my first note that night.

David Bowie, an artist who needs no introduction, was in New York, meeting with people from EMI/Capitol, his record label. They wanted to take him out to celebrate his new album, *Let's Dance*, but David said he was busy that night. He told them he was going to see his favorite singer at the Ritz . . . and his favorite singer was *me*!

David's recommendation started a stampede. Suddenly, Roger was bombarded by calls from music executives who were desperate to get tickets to the show that night. Ironically, Capitol had been one of my labels, but I became infinitely more interesting to them after I got David's seal of approval. I didn't know any of this until later. When I walked out onto the stage, the room was packed and vibrating. It was my favorite kind of show—great energy and an audience that was with me every high-kicking step of the way. I spotted some famous faces in the crowd, including tennis great John McEnroe and actress Susan Sarandon.

David, who had my old friend Keith Richards in tow, came backstage to my dressing room, and they were all so excited about the show. I was really happy that I had performed David's "Putting Out Fire," the song he wrote for the movie *Cat People*. I think I did a good job covering it with my band, and it meant something to me that he was there to hear it. The three of us were having such a great time talking about music (and passing around bottles of Jack Daniel's and champagne) that we didn't want the night to end. We moved the party to Keith's suite at the Plaza Hotel. At that point, I had the most fun watching Roger's reactions as the night unfolded. He was over the moon. I think if it had been possible for him to faint, he would have, he was flying so high, thrilled to be in the company of his idols.

David was playing the piano, Keith was in top form, Ron Wood dropped by, and we jammed the night away. We sang, "I keep forgetting you don't love me no more," which David said he was planning to put on his new album. Roger kept popping into the other room to use the telephone. Like an excited kid, he was calling his friends to say, "You'll never guess where I am! You'll never guess who's with me!" It meant so much to him for all those people to be there. It was a rock 'n' roll dream. We didn't leave until early morning, when we hailed a taxi and headed back to reality.

A *new* reality, as it turned out. Getting back to my Cinderella tale: for me, that night at the Ritz was the equivalent of going to the ball (minus the part about Prince Charming) because it changed my life dramatically. Buoyed by the enthusiasm they witnessed at my show,

Capitol wanted to move ahead with a record deal. It got very complicated trying to work something out between Capitol in America and
EMI in England, but Roger was like a warrior manager when it came
to making things happen. Against all odds, we found ourselves walking into Abbey Road Studios (by way of a quick, moneymaking concert in Sweden) for a recording session with Martyn Ware and Glenn
Gregory of the innovative pop-techno group Heaven 17. Martyn, who
was practically a boy, though a very talented one, happened to think
that this middle-aged singer had a bright future.

I walked into the studio expecting to see musicians. Weirdly,
there wasn't a human or an instrument in sight. "Where's the band?"
I asked, thinking back to Phil Spector and his giant orchestra. Roger
and Martyn explained that the new Wall of Sound would come from
something that looked like a giant X-ray machine. Martyn created
his music with synthesizers. I was a little puzzled by the process, but
happy and excited to take a chance on something new, even if it meant
singing along with a machine. The problem was, what would I sing?
There was no time for Martyn to write new material, so we talked
about songs we liked and agreed to try David Bowie's "1984" and Al
Green's "Let's Stay Together."

The first time I hear a song, I start singing along until I feel that I
have it, exactly the way I did it as a child, when I listened to the radio.
When I've absorbed it fully, I say, "Okay, it's my song now, I own it,"
and I'm ready to record. I go to the studio, step up to the microphone,
and get it done. I'm different from most artists in that respect. When
I make a record, I like to sing a song all the way through, from start to
finish. To me, it's a story, with a beginning, a middle, and an end, and
it has to be told in its entirety.

When I recorded "Let's Stay Together," I had a crush on some-one back in America, so I did it as a love song. That's why my version was so different from Al Green's. Al wrote the song, loves the music, and all of that. But I was coming from a more emotional place. As I finished the last lyric, Martyn called it a wrap. We got it in one take. Sometimes they call me the "one-take wonder." The song was blessed, and it continued to be blessed when my recording of it came out in England, and later in America. It was a hit!

When you've been in the record business as long as I was with Ike, it's impossible not to be suspicious of success. When I was told I had a hit record, I thought, *Okay, fine*. But I didn't wake up and think, *Oh, I guess I'm a star . . . again*. And there was a downside. A few of my girls quit when I told them I couldn't afford to give them raises. "The song just hit," I tried to explain. "The money's not even here yet." Fortunately, "Let's Stay Together" was enough of a hit for my record company to tell Roger to move forward with producing a new album. And they wanted it done as quickly as possible.

Roger and I headed back to London, where I'd found support and inspiration from the earliest days of my career, starting with "River Deep—Mountain High." The English people stepped up for me when America didn't. They never asked, "Where's Ike?" They accepted me as a solo artist. You know those old Hollywood movies, when talented kids get together and spontaneously put on a show—the way I used to do with my cousins at Mama Georgie's house back in Nutbush? That's what it felt like when we set out to make the *Private Dancer* album. Ac-tually, we didn't know the song "Private Dancer" at first. We started out with one song, "Better Be Good to Me," by Holly Knight. The stu-dio was booked—we had two and a half weeks to record an entire album—and Roger raced around town in a small car with a big bag of cassettes, frantically gathering potential material—something, anything, for me to sing. It was a funny way to begin a project.

Roger brought me a demo of "What's Love Got to Do with It," and we immediately clashed because I didn't like the song, not one bit. "What am I going to do with it?" I said dismissively. It was certainly not what Rod Stewart or the Rolling Stones would sing, I argued. Roger disagreed. He prided himself on his ability to spot a hit, and he thought this song was a smash. Asking me to please keep an open mind, Roger took me to the studio to meet with the songwriter, Terry Britten, whom he had already asked to produce two songs on the album. Terry was sitting casually on a stool, swinging his legs and holding his guitar. I told him he looked just like a little boy, which thankfully he took with good humor.

Terry talked to me about the song and listened to my concerns. He understood what I was saying—I didn't want to do something light, or pop. Then I decided to show him some respect. I sang his words, but did it *my* way: "You must understand that the touch of your hand . . . ," forcefully, with gravity and raw emotion. Oh yeah. It was a whole different approach, and a whole different outcome. I heard in my voice what Roger was imagining in his head. The album was off to a great start, and Terry Britten and I enjoyed a long, happy collaboration.

Meanwhile, Roger was still running all over London, looking for more songs. Mark Knopfler of Dire Straits said he had one called "Private Dancer." He'd written it for himself, but hadn't used it on his most recent album because he decided it was a song that was better for a woman than a man. He was absolutely right. I can't even describe how "Private Dancer" sounded coming from a man, even a very talented man like Mark. Very butch! Like something you'd hear in a pub, after too many pints had been consumed. "Do you really want me to sing this song?" I said to Roger, half-amused, half-appalled. "You just put your touch on it and we'll see how it goes," he answered reassuringly. And that's what I did.

The song is about prostitution. I never had to stoop to that in my life, but I think most of us have been in situations where we had to sell ourselves, one way or another. When I gave into Ike, when I kept quiet to avoid an argument, when I stayed with him despite longing to leave, that's what I was thinking about when I sang the song, the sadness of doing something that you don't want to do, day in, day out. It's very emotional.

We found more songs, including "Steel Claw," with Jeff Beck on guitar, "I Can't Stand the Rain," "Better Be Good to Me," and others—all memorable to me because I was doing what I loved, in a city I loved, and with people who genuinely cared about me and my future. There were so many times in my life when I felt I had to rise above bad karma. But, when I was making *Private Dancer*, life showered me with good karma. I am constantly amazed by my fellow artists. They were busy with their own work, but didn't they all make time for me, and my album? The experience really proved that musicians are incredibly generous. They wanted to lift me, not bring me down.

And I was lifted higher and higher from the moment the *Private Dancer* album was released. During the summer of 1984, I was on the road with Lionel Ritchie (I was his opening act on the *Can't Slow Down* tour), when "What's Love Got to Do with It" started to climb the charts. How exciting it was to have people sing along with me when I performed it or "Let's Stay Together" onstage.

I discovered that the music business was changing in ways I'd never anticipated. It wasn't enough to record and release a song. With MTV, the new twenty-four-hour cable channel that had become so popular, artists had to make little films—music videos—to illustrate their songs. The first one we did was for "Let's Stay Together." As Roger liked to say, the production was "cheap and cheerful"—just me and my dancers, Annie and Lejeune, a camera, and a tiny budget of two thousand dollars. It created quite a stir because when people saw the three of us dancing close they thought it was a little naughty. We had a good laugh over that.

We tried something different with "What's Love Got to Do with It." We shot one version in black-and-white—a little artsy—but my record company thought it looked too serious. Later that summer, while I was in New York performing at the Ritz again, we took our cameras to the streets. I was filmed strutting through Brooklyn and lower Manhattan, wearing what has become an iconic look for me—a denim jacket, miniskirt, heels, big hair, and red, red lips. The video was a huge success and went on to win an MTV Video Music Award in 1985.

Suddenly, we were shooting music videos for every song, so I did get to release my inner actress. I don't know where we found the time. The one we did for "Private Dancer" was really ambitious, with fantasy sequences, dances choreographed by Arlene Phillips, five or six costume changes for me, and a wonderful location, the old Rivoli Ballroom in London.

I don't think I ever stopped moving during this time.

Of course, I was excited about my best-selling records, but my favorite part of my success (which was years too late to be seen as happening overnight) was the avalanche of opportunities that came my way because of it. Every time I had a chance to collaborate with a great singer, songwriter, or producer, or to try a different kind of music, I was becoming a better artist.

Take Bryan Adams, for example. He was so young when I met him in 1984—twenty-four, I think—and adorable. He had this glint in his eye, just like Dennis the Menace. Bryan claimed to have been a fan of mine for years (although he didn't look old enough to have done anything for years) and said that when he was a teenager he came to see me at the clubs where I did my cabaret act. He sent me tapes of songs that he wanted me to do, but they were never right. Not that rejection kept him from trying. He was very persistent, and I'm glad he was.

When I heard "It's Only Love" the first time, I knew it was the song for me. Bryan came on as producer, the record was a hit, and we had such a good time performing it together that I invited him to come on tour with me. I introduced him as "a guy from Canada"—the audience immediately knew who I was talking about—and added "He's really cute, you know," because he was! Bryan had such great energy when he opened the show that he made me want to come out singing and dancing—which was exactly what the Rolling Stones said about Ike and Tina back in the 1960s.

I'd been interested in doing more acting ever since I did *Tommy*, so imagine how flattered I was when Steven Spielberg approached me about playing Shug Avery, one of the lead roles in *The Color Purple*, but I just couldn't bring myself to do it. As worthy as the project was, it just didn't feel right to me. The story was uncomfortably close to the story of my life with Ike. Did I say close? It was practically next door! I didn't want to relive any of that nightmare ever again, even on screen.

Mad Max: Beyond Thunderdome was a completely different kind of film. I'm told that when the producers were discussing casting ideas for "Aunty Entity," the strong, larger-than-life heroine at the center of their futuristic action/adventure film, they kept saying "Let's get someone like Tina Turner"—they actually referred to her as "the Tina Turner character." Finally, it occurred to someone to ask the *real* Tina if she would consider taking on the role.

I had seen the two previous *Mad Max* movies and was a huge fan of director George Miller's work, especially *Road Warrior*. He made my heart beat a little faster when he offered me the part. This was my type of acting! I didn't want to do Hollywood, because Hollywood is all about glamour and beauty, and I never saw myself as a beauty. I was still a tomboy at heart. The thought of traveling halfway around the world to the wilds of central Australia, shaving my head, wearing armor, and driving in fast cars, not to mention playing a queen . . . Are you kidding? This was a dream come true. Of course, I wasn't thinking about the dust, or the heat—that the temperature would rise higher than 125 degrees, so high that it made it difficult to fill the gas tanks on the stunt cars because the fuel evaporated as soon as it hit the air! I was thinking about the fabulous character and the realization of one of my favorite fantasies: playing a woman who has the power of a man.

I really connected with Entity. I can be many different women at different times—sexy, jolly, silly, younger than my age, wise beyond my years. But the woman at my core is very much like Entity, strong and resilient. She lost so much, and then she went through so much to get the men in her world to respect her. I related to her struggles because I lived them.

The physical process of transforming myself from Tina into Entity was very interesting. I learned how to shave my own head every day, because the skin is so tender that it's better if you do it yourself. I was surprised to see that my face was very, very nice with a shaven head. I was a little worried about that. Then, the hair and makeup people came in to build the look, which was topped off by a wild blond wig. Finally, they put the gear on me. My armor weighed seventy pounds and was made of chicken wire, dog muzzles, and who knows what else. Oh my God, I looked fierce.

The costume department did an amazing job, but I didn't trust them to get the shoes right. No one ever does. I brought my own heels to the set, designer heels I knew I could really stand in (good thing, because I had to wear them for hours at a time). At the end of each prep, I was sprayed with all sorts of finishing stuff, and when the team was done, Tina was gone. I was Aunty Entity, from head to toe.

Because I'm a little bit daring, I insisted on doing my own stunts. Even I have to admit it was scary at times. *Beyond Thunderdome* had some wild scenes. On a movie set, the trick is to work with the crew to protect yourself from getting hurt. For example, I was supposed to make a dramatic jump while wearing high heels. I took one look at the drop (this is the same person who didn't think twice before jumping off a stage when she was eight months pregnant) and decided I was guaranteed to twist my ankle. I told them we needed a box to break the jump—and I took off the shoes while I was jumping and put them back on for the shot of me landing. Ah . . . the magic of moviemaking.

I was responsible for Entity's signature laugh. George Miller heard me laughing on the set one day—I think someone's hat had blown away and landed under a truck, or something silly like that—and he decided that Entity had to sound just like me—playful and sinister at the same time.

One of my favorite pastimes was sitting behind George to watch him while he was directing the other actors. I wanted to see what the movie world was really like. He'd say, "You are the most focused singer/actress I've ever seen." I think he was surprised to find that I worked easily with others: that I wasn't a prima donna. I wanted to tell him, "You don't know where I came from! No prima donnas allowed." When I look back, I see that I'm not terrific in the movie, not as good as I'd like to have been. But I did my best, and I guess I'm good enough.

I was charmed by my costar, Mel Gibson, whom I always called "Melvin," because he had a little boy quality that reminded me of one of my sons. He's very loose and playful. Working with him was very much like working with musicians—you have a good time, but you get the job done. I developed such an affection for him that, after the movie was finished, it troubled me to read stories about his bad behavior. I knew that Melvin was better than that, so I sent him a picture of himself with the note, "Please don't mess this up." He took my words seriously and was happy that I was supportive and concerned about his well-being.

I can't help mothering the people I care about. I've always been that way. Keith Richards described me perfectly when he told *Vanity Fair* that he saw me as a "favorite aunt" or a "fairy godmother," because I was always trying to take care of people when we were on the road. If anyone had a cold, I'd nag them to button up their coat and wear a scarf, and I'd offer VapoRub for sore throats. At heart, I'm equal parts "Mother Earth" and "Rock 'n' Roll," and I think that's why my friendships with others in the business have endured.

The wild and wonderful ride that started with *Private Dancer* culminated at the 1984 Grammy Awards, which took place on the night of February 26, 1985. I was feeling a little woozy because I had the flu, but even if I had been in the best of health the evening would have been an out-of-body experience. When I entered the stage at the top of a flight of stairs and walked down singing "What's Love Got to Do with It," I felt the warm embrace of the audience. They loved the song, but they also loved the story that came with it. I think I spoke to all the people who dream of getting a second chance and work tirelessly to make that dream come true. Roger was with me that night, but neither of us imagined that "What's Love Got to Do with It" would win two Grammys, one for Record of the Year and one for Best Female Pop Vocal Performance, and "Better Be Good to Me" would win yet a third award, for Best Female Rock Vocal Performance.

The *Private Dancer* album went on to sell eight million copies in its first year.

Don't worry, Roger, we'll be fine.

It's funny for me to remember the first flush of my new success. There was no time to stop and think about what I was doing—between making *Beyond Thunderdome*, fulfilling individual concert obligations, and setting out on the first leg of the *Private Dancer* tour, I traveled constantly, rarely touching ground. I didn't even have a chance to get a credit card, although that didn't stop the newly affluent me from becoming a world-class shopper. Actually, I was always a world-class shopper, but now I could afford it! In one of my "Tina Turner Comeback" interviews, I told *People* that all I wanted was an American Express Gold card. Until such time that I could get my hands on one, I borrowed a credit card from my manager and anyone else in my orbit. "Don't worry," I assured the interviewer. "I always pay them back."

———

About a month after the Grammy Awards, I performed a duet with David Bowie. I still get goose bumps when I think about it. David and I stayed close after that night at the Ritz. We developed a special friendship—a togetherness that came from mutual affection and admiration, and shared interests. He, like me, was a Buddhist. He joked that at a certain point in his life, he had to choose between becoming a Buddhist monk or a rock 'n' roll star. I'd listen to him speak and ask, "David, how do you know so much?" because he was smart about everything—not just music—*everything.* He could talk about art, religion, any topic. He'd laugh and say, "Tina, I never stop studying." He was a student of life, a real Renaissance man, but not in a heavy way. When I think of David, I think of a beam of light. He practically had a halo.

The music video we made of his song "Tonight," which was filmed during a live performance at the NEC Arena in Birmingham, England, in March 1985, says everything about our feelings for each other. I began by singing *"Everything's gonna be all right, tonight,"* swaying to the seductive reggae beat of the music. Then David appeared, stepping out of the mist wearing a short white tuxedo jacket. The audience was surprised, and the place vibrated as if an earthquake had struck! He looked so beautiful, like an angel. I wanted to say "Wow!" but I couldn't speak. I had to do something other than stand there, so I did a dramatic double take. Who wouldn't at the sight of such a vision?

While we were rehearsing the night before, I had made some discoveries about David. He really knew how to dance, and he knew how to act. Not all singers do. When we embraced on that stage, it was a wonderful moment. We looked transported, like a couple in love. Although, contrary to rumors—and I hate to disappoint anyone here—

we never had *that* kind of relationship. We never even slept together. David was different from other rockers. He was a real gentleman.

I might as well move on to the next hot topic. One of the most debated questions in the history of rock 'n' roll, and I don't think I'm exaggerating here because I get asked this question *all* the time, is "What did David Bowie whisper in your ear when you were dancing together in the 'Tonight' video?" Journalists and fans beg for the answer. Some have suggested they might bring in a lip reader to decipher David's words, but his mouth is so close to my ear and his lips are not completely visible, so that won't help.

To recap: David leans in and whispers, and I react as if I've heard something very naughty. No, he did not say anything smutty. I definitely would remember that. But I'm trying to recall what he *did* say to me.

The truth is, I just don't remember. And now that David has gone to his grave, his words will have to remain a mystery—although there's no guarantee that his memory would have been any better than mine. He probably forgot, too.

At some point during our duet, a young woman came running up onto the stage and grabbed David by the arm. It happened fast—the guards removed her, and David, who had a wonderful sense of humor and was quick-witted, immediately joked something like "I guess I should be glad it was a girl"—meaning that the press always made such a big deal about his sexuality, they'd have had a field day if a man had done something like that. Today, they wouldn't say anything, or they'd describe him as being sexually "fluid," but at the time, it was a big story, and that amused him.

After "Tonight," I mentioned to David that I wanted him to write a song for me, something similar to the feeling of "Putting Out Fire." He said yes, but I doubted that he'd get around to doing it. Artists often said yes to me, and they meant well, but then they'd go off and get involved with their own lives and forget about it. Not David. He called me a few months later, while he was skiing somewhere, and said that he had a great song for me, "It's called 'Girls,'" he told me, describing it as "really rough," just the way I liked it. "And," he added, "if you don't take it, I'm going to do it."

"Wait a second," I said. "If *you* want it, that means it's right."

Sometimes, when people try to write a song specifically for me, it doesn't work. I tell them, you don't understand, I can relate to what *you* relate to. If I hear that they've written it for themselves, and that *they* would sing it, then I'll take it. As soon as David expressed a desire to sing "Girls" (and he did end up recording it), I knew it was a good song, a universal song. I love what it says about women, that they're powerful and mysterious. It took me a little while to understand it when I was getting ready to record it, but that's what I love about David's music, it always makes me think.

The last time I saw David, he was performing in Brussels. I stopped by his dressing room after the concert and we caught up with each other. Our visit was sweet, although he was so secretive about being sick that I didn't know it was our "last dance," our final goodbye.

"Love you, Tina," he said.

"Love you, David," I answered.

I'm so glad those were our parting words.

Erwin, who knows the music business inside out because it's been his profession his entire adult life, once asked me, "Why did Bowie and Jagger take you under their wing? They didn't do that for anybody else." I explained to him that the English were appreciative of me from the early "Ike and Tina" days, and they became even more supportive after I left Ike.

I think they saw something they liked—a woman who could stand up to them vocally, collaborate onstage in a rock 'n' roll way, and make it all look like great fun. David always said, "When you're dancing with Tina, she looks you in the eye." We were partners. Equals. At the time, there were no women who sang and danced like me—women who could be sexy without making it sexual. I went out in high-heeled shoes and a short dress, and there was good dancing and laughter and fun, without making the women in the audience feel like I was after their men. There was never anything coming from the stage that was negative. Beyoncé has that same kind of energy today, but I was the only one back then.

How many women can hold up their end of the stage with Mick Jagger? Yet Mick and I always had the best time together, and our performance at Live Aid in 1985, the historic concert organized by Bob Geldof to raise money for the famine in Ethiopia, is a perfect example.

It was late in the evening at JFK Stadium in Philadelphia. The temperature reached ninety-five degrees, and the audience had been there all day, listening to everyone from Tom Petty and Madonna to the Beach Boys and Bob Dylan. Now they were waiting for Mick, who wasn't about to let extreme heat stop him from giving his usual high-energy performance. He was always very physical (although I always smiled when I remembered his impromptu dance classes with me and the Ikettes back in London). That's what his fans expected to see.

I was making a surprise appearance that night to sing two songs with Mick, and before we went onstage, we spoke briefly about the tempo. Hall & Oates were playing backup for Mick, who was working as a solo artist, without the Rolling Stones, and I was concerned that they were playing a little slow. I need momentum. I can't dance to slow. I said, "Mick, I don't know if this is going to work if they can't pick it up." He told me not to worry, that he would take care of it. "I know what you want," he said. "You want it *fast*." And he went out and talked to the band about picking it up.

When he came back, he asked me, "So, what are we going to *do*?" Mick and I could never just stand there and sing. That wasn't us. We had to *do* something. He looked me over—I was wearing a tight-fitting black leather top and skirt—and I could see a naughty idea forming.

"Does that skirt come off?" he asked slyly.

"What!" was my startled reply.

"I'm going to take your skirt off."

I asked him why, but it was too late to talk it through. Mick had already made up his mind to do it. "Just to create something," he said. Understandably, I was a little nervous because I'd never had my skirt taken off onstage. Luckily, I was prepared. In those days especially, you didn't just wear undies. I wore fishnet stockings over my underwear, then dancer's briefs over that—if my skirt came off, there would be nothing to see except a costume *under* a costume—I was covered, I reassured myself. And Mick knew I was covered. We were professionals.

Mick walked onto the stage, thanked the audience for bearing up under the heat, and then called, "Where's Tina?" I came out and we went right into "State of Shock." It was good, but a little too tame for Mick, who likes a lot of excitement. When we started "It's Only Rock 'n' Roll," he pulled off his shirt, danced around bare-chested, then sashayed off the stage to change into a yellow jacket and camouflage pants, singing, "*But I like it,*" the whole time.

He came back, and without missing a beat, he reached for my waist. I felt—oh my God, I felt him feeling around where the snap was. I knew it was going to happen. I glanced down because I wondered, how did I look at that moment? When he pulled off my skirt with a flourish, I saw with relief that it wasn't bad. Thanks to the dancer's briefs holding me in like a girdle, and the fishnet stockings hiding my underwear, everything was in shape and in place, like a dancer. I managed to appear startled—that's the actress in me—and I ducked behind Mick to make it really look like it was a surprise. The audience loved it.

Mick is just naughty, you know? We just play. The first time I appeared onstage with him, he tried to press the microphone in my crotch. He's like every bad boy you've ever known at school. That's why I always think of the Rolling Stones as boys, because I've raised sons. When you raise boys, you know they are playful. I always had to be on guard with Mick because I never knew what prank was coming next. But he's like a brother. It wasn't as if some random guy pulled off my skirt. It was like a boy I knew did it . . . a very old "boy."

Mick has a quick wit. I remember that right after I left Ike, I visited Mick in his dressing room after a show, and when he saw me he teased, "I don't want any liberated women in here." I could tell that he was happy for me, and that he wanted to acknowledge the important changes in my life, but he did it his way, with a dry, humorous twist.

A year after Live Aid, I ran into Mick at the Prince's Trust concert at Wembley Arena in London. Conversation between us is always like a game of Ping-Pong because he likes to compete, compete, compete. I said something like, "Oh Mick, your hair looks so good." Without pausing for a second, he answered back, "Yes, and it's *mine*." That's Mick, pointing out the difference between my wig and his natural locks. No one can outtalk him. That's why he gives the best interviews. He knows how to have fun with journalists—how to turn the questions around and throw them right back at the person asking, so he always comes out on top.

No matter how much he teased me, Mick and the other Stones have always been there when I needed them. I know we're friends. I know we can depend on each other. Meanwhile, for the rest of our lives, Mick and I will continue teasing each other and being playful. That's our way.

I had the most wonderful times when my solo career took flight. I could literally count my blessings—and I did—following the *Private Dancer* album: touring with the Rolling Stones, Rod Stewart, Lionel Ritchie, and Bryan Adams; making a Mad Max movie with Mel Gibson; the Grammys; recording a duet with David Bowie—I enjoyed artistic freedom and commercial success.

When I left Ike, I gathered all the awards we had won together and put them away. I said to myself, "All right, I'm going to see what I can do on my own." I went on to fill the empty spaces with new awards, certificates, and silver, platinum, and triple platinum albums. People called me an "overnight sensation." Of course, there is no such thing, but there *are* second acts. The second time around, I had the opportunity to rewrite my life—to do it all over again, as I wanted—without having to live in the shadow of someone else. Ike always told me that I was holding him back. But I realized it was just the opposite. With every blow to my body—and to my self-esteem—he was holding *me* back. Without Ike, I could soar.

Mark Knopfler summed it up perfectly when he wrote the song "Overnight Sensation" for me. We were in Canada at the time. He caught my performance, and, that night, as he watched me closely, the idea came to him to write a song about a girl who's been out there a long time. She's been in the badlands, yet she never stopped dreaming. When Mark first gave me the song I thought, *Do I want to sing this? Do I want to be reminded of Ike, and how bad it was until I left him?* Mark's song helped me understand that it was the road I'd had to take—that what happened was my destiny. Ike would always be a part of my story, but he was becoming the receding image in the rearview mirror. I had to think about the future, not the past.

After I started working with Roger, Ike asked our sons to approach me about going out on the road with him one more time. He even spoke to Roger. I think he had some crazy idea about teaming up with Sonny & Cher on an "exes tour," if you can imagine that. I said to Roger, "Are you nuts? You have no idea what you would be dealing with if we worked with Ike. He's a con man, and that's not even the worst thing I could say about him." I couldn't bear the thought of standing on a stage with Ike, let alone consider singing his music.

I didn't have to worry about confrontations with Ike for very long. The bigger my success, the quieter he became. That's strange, isn't it? After "What's Love Got to Do with It" hit number 1 on the charts, there were no more appeals for a reunion of any kind. I think Ike finally realized that I wasn't coming back.

I never heard from Ike Turner again.

Not a single word up to the day he died on December 12, 2007.

—

8

"FOREIGN AFFAIR"

> **There's romance
> in the air,
> so they say**
>
> **Love could be a
> small café away**

As I told poor Roger over and over again, probably until he was sick of hearing it—my long-held dream was to pack a stadium or a giant arena, just like the Rolling Stones. That dream came true with the 1985 *Private Dancer* tour. We did 180 shows in ten months, traveling the world to locations in North America, Europe, Australia, and Asia. Over two million people came to see the "new Tina," the solo artist now known for "What's Love Got to Do with It," "Let's Stay Together," and "Private Dancer." But I still sang their old favorites, especially "Proud Mary" and "River Deep—Mountain High," and the audience loved hearing them. *Billboard* magazine wrote, "She comes to give," and that's exactly how I felt. I was thrilled to be on that stage. "Are you ready for me?" I'd ask the crowd. Boy, were they *ready*! It was hard work, but I gave it my all, from when I came out kicking, right up to the last encore, which was usually my version of the ZZ Top song "Legs."

Speaking of legs, *Billboard* also said that I had "the most kinetic legs in the business." I was—and I am still—amused by the constant attention paid to my legs. I truly don't get the fuss. Did you ever see a pony's legs when it's just born? Long and spindly? That's what my legs always looked like to me. When I was young, I used to think, "Why do I look like a little pony?" My short torso is hooked onto these two little dangling legs, but I've learned how to wear clothes to flatter them. In Nutbush, no one would have looked twice at my legs. Black women who were full and curvy were considered beautiful, but my body, which was just skinny and straight, never turned any heads. I know how to make myself look good, but I wouldn't call myself a pretty woman.

Being on tour for almost a year left me with very little time for a personal life. I'd been without a serious boyfriend for ages. Not that I ever had a lot of men in my life—I spent my entire youth with Ike—and, after my divorce, dating was often more trouble than it was worth. I was never one of those women who had to have sex no matter what. There have been times when I've gone up to a year without it, to be honest. If you saw me on a man's arm, it meant something. I didn't go out with men just to have companionship. There were a few infatuations here and there, but nothing important. Don't laugh, but I'd always been a little nervous about starting a relationship with a new man because I didn't know how my wig would be received!

The wig is a critical part of the Tina Turner look. If I walked out onstage with "natural" hair, the audience wouldn't recognize me. They'd say, "Where's Tina?" I once went to a doctor in St. Louis who actually asked me about my race while he was taking my medical history. When I said, "Black," he argued with me. "Your hair," he pointed out incredulously, noting that it was straight and lustrous. He had no idea I was wearing a wig, and that's a reaction I get all the time.

I'm not surprised when people think my wig is my own hair, because I've always considered it to be an extension of myself. In a way, it *is* my hair. When I was performing, I never wanted the wig to become like a costume—some entertainers change wigs the way they change clothes—so I kept my look consistent. If my "hair" was curly offstage, I used the same basic style and color onstage: I just made it look more dramatic. "I prepare it like a three-course meal," I used to say in the eighties, when high hair was "in." I washed it, let it dry, forked it up, added gooey stuff, and forked it up and let it dry again. It was exaggerated, but it worked. When I was onstage, I handled the hair as if it were my own, flipping it, running my hands through it, and pushing it away from my face. The way I tossed that hair when I danced was so realistic that no one could be absolutely certain it wasn't, as Mick liked to say, *mine*.

I will never stop wearing a wig. But as much as I loved the convenience and easy beauty it gave me, I always ran the risk of meeting a man who might object: a man who would have a problem becoming romantically involved with *Tina*, with her bountiful hair and glamorous trimmings, but waking up with unadorned Anna Mae. What if he was disappointed by the real me? I was always a bit nervous about taking that chance.

This dilemma wasn't a pressing concern, because I was working so hard on the *Private Dancer* tour that I really didn't have time for a boyfriend. At least, that's what I told myself until the day Roger and I flew into Cologne for a big show. I was tired and a little down, thinking of the grueling schedule ahead. As we walked through the airport, a young man stepped out from behind a column to greet us. I thought he was a stranger, maybe a fan, but Roger recognized him right away and greeted him warmly, saying "Hello, Erwin." He was Erwin Bach, an executive from EMI, my record company in Europe, and he was there to deliver a surprise from Roger, a new Mercedes jeep, the hard-to-get G-Wagon. But the real surprise wasn't the car, it was the man!

Apparently, the keys this charismatic stranger held in his hand were to my heart, which suddenly started to beat BOOM, BOOM, BOOM, drowning out all other sounds. My hands were ice-cold. My body was shaking inside. *This is what they call love at first sight*, I marveled. All I could think—if I could think at all—was, *Oh my God, I am not ready for this.* The heartthrob in front of me held out his arms and said hello. I thought, *Well I'm not going into those arms*, although I wanted to, but I didn't trust myself. We finished our introductions and pleasantries and walked out of the airport. Roger hopped into our waiting limousine, while I got into the G-Wagon with Erwin so he could tell me all about it while driving me to the hotel.

I studied him from the side while we were driving. He was young—about thirty, I guessed—and he was very pretty, although not in a conventional way. He had dark hair and really great hands. There's something about a man's hands I like. Suddenly, I felt very insecure about my own looks. I was wearing an Issey Miyake sweater with leather jeans—rock 'n' roll stuff—and while I was very colorful, when I look back I'm sure it was not my best moment. My hair was Big, Big, Big in those days, big and wild. I had just forked and teased it, like that proverbial three-course meal, so it was sticking out. That was my style, it was what people expected to see. But if you ask me, I didn't look so good and I doubt that Erwin found me attractive. Oh, and if the hair wasn't enough of a turn-off, I was forty-six, divorced, and the mother of two—really four—"children" who, if I was being completely honest, were practically men . . . just like Erwin.

What was going through Erwin's mind? Later, much later, I found out that he was feeling the same inexplicable electrical charge that passed through me. He described our meeting as being magical, and claimed that when he looked at me, he didn't see the "star," or my skin color, or any other details. He saw a woman—a very desirable woman, but he didn't know what to do with his feelings.

Our conversation was a little strained in the G-Wagon. I was having trouble focusing (apparently, he was, too), and there was a bit of a language barrier. Erwin was extremely well educated and knew English, but he hadn't been speaking it a lot, so there were some awkward silences. *Snap back*, I told myself during the ride that was weirdly both too short and too long. *Speak!* Desperate for something to say, I asked him to show me the switch for the fog lights (as if that were a real question), and he blushed as he tried to find it. We managed to chat haltingly about the dashboard and other innocuous subjects until we got to the hotel.

I said goodbye, and still shaking, I made it upstairs to my room, threw myself on the bed, and thought, *Gosh, he's wonderful*. Really *wonderful. What do I do now?* I was shocked. I'd had no idea that I would find swoony, love-at-first-sight love in Germany. I almost had the sense that we'd connected in another life. Now I had to figure out how to connect in *this* life.

I call making things happen "knitting," and I'm very good at it. The next night, I was at a dinner with the EMI team, including Erwin. I announced that I was having a Christmas party (a decision I had made that very moment) and they were all invited (yes, I'd just thought of that, too). Then, in a real stroke of genius, I added, "Okay, everybody. I want your birth dates so I can have your astrological charts done to get to know you better." There was only one person I wanted to know better—Erwin—and the more I learned about him (one psychic warned me that you can't tell him what to do—which is absolutely true to this day), the more I was attracted to him. It didn't matter that he was younger, or that he lived in Europe. You know what I think? I think I needed love. I really needed to love a person. I was a free woman, free to choose. And I chose Erwin.

———

I was kind of naughty in those early days. One night, when we were sitting next to each other at yet another business dinner, I said to myself, *I don't care. I'm just going to ask him.* I looked at him—so handsome in his Lacoste shirt, jeans, and loafers without socks—and whispered, "Erwin, when you come to America, I want you to make love to me." He turned his head slowly and just looked at me, as if he couldn't believe his ears. I couldn't believe what I had said either! Later, he told me he had never heard that from a woman. His first thought was *Wow, those California girls are really wild.* But I wasn't wild. I'd never done anything remotely like that before. I didn't recognize myself.

Eventually, Erwin came to Los Angeles on business, and there was a dinner at Spago, Wolfgang Puck's famous see-and-be-seen restaurant. I invited everyone back to my house after dinner (another one of my not-so-subtle contrivances), and that's when our real romance began. The music was playing, the other guests drifted away, the kissing began, and we kissed all the way to the bedroom. Erwin stayed with me that night.

Remember, I'd never had much experience with love or courtship. My first crush in high school ended in heartbreak. I was still a teenager when I had my first adult relationship, with Raymond, my son Craig's father. And then there was my marriage to Ike, and you know how that went. It took me decades to start behaving like a lovesick schoolgirl, and I was enjoying the roller-coaster ride of emotions that came with my second adolescence.

The next morning, Erwin was scheduled to go to Hawaii on a business trip. I dropped him off at his hotel and drove home, on cloud nine the whole way. When Rhonda, who was always behind a camera, brought me some pictures of the two of us at dinner the night before,

I immediately slipped them into frames and displayed them around the house. Erwin was in my thoughts for the next two days . . . until he called and casually mentioned that the trip to Hawaii had been canceled. He was a few miles away in Malibu—he'd been there the whole time, hanging out at the beach with his colleagues, and hadn't thought to tell me. I tried to stay cool, but inside I was furious. "Tina, you stupid old fool," I fumed at myself. Why did I make such bad choices in men? Why was there always disappointment? I couldn't bear the thought of being hurt again. I was better off alone, I decided.

A few months passed. I ran into Erwin when I was promoting *Private Dancer* in Basel, Switzerland, and got that old feeling. I had rented a house in Gstaad for the holidays, and I invited Erwin and some other people from the EMI team to visit. One night, I was sitting by the fireplace with my friend Harriet, when I said wistfully, "Oh, I wish Erwin were here." He had made such a deep impression on me that I couldn't stop thinking about him. But I wasn't very hopeful about him joining me in Gstaad. Harriet said, "Be careful what you wish, honey. You just might get it." I'm not sure if she knew something, or if she was a little bit psychic, but suddenly, my security guard called up to say, "Tina, someone's here to see you." When I went to the door, there was Erwin. The universe had given me exactly what I wanted. How did I feel? Happy. Excited. Nervous. Ready.

Erwin was wearing a little country hat that's popular in Germany—funny, but cute. In a rush, I remembered that I liked everything about him, including his funny hat. Erwin exuded a masculinity that I found irresistible. There was the roguishness of a boy, and the wisdom and composure of an older man: a great combination. And now, because he was *here*, on my doorstep, I knew that he liked me. By the end of the evening, our fates were sealed. I made up my mind to pack up and move in with him during my upcoming vacation. From now on, wherever Erwin was would be my home.

Before we could begin a public relationship, there was something Erwin insisted on doing. He was always extremely professional about his position at EMI. When Erwin graduated from college, his father encouraged him to accept a job with a steel company, which promised to offer him a solid, if unexciting, future. The problem was that Erwin had come across an advertisement for a position at a music company that asked, "Do you want to work with the Beatles?" Well, of course he wanted to work with the Beatles. He loved music and was enthusiastic about turning a passion into a profession. He responded to the ad, which had been placed by EMI, was hired, and began his career in the music business, ultimately achieving such success that even his father had to admit that he was right to choose the Beatles over steel.

Erwin didn't think it was appropriate to date an EMI artist (namely me) without discussing the idea with his superiors. He made an appointment to see Sir Wilfried Jung, EMI's managing director for Central Europe, to explain the situation. Erwin was nervous because he couldn't predict what the reaction would be. What if he had to choose between his job and me? He presented his situation to Sir Wilfried, who listened attentively and appeared to be thinking. Finally, he spoke.

"There is a problem," offered Sir Wilfried.

"May I know what that problem is?" Erwin asked respectfully.

"I could become a little jealous," Sir Wilfried answered, which was his way of giving Erwin his blessing.

He had one caveat. "Listen," he cautioned Erwin. "If this is real—

if it's a romance—that's great. But don't let me read in the paper next week that it's over." With these words, Erwin was free to move forward. Thus began my love story.

I'm going to back up for a moment to discuss the elephant in the room—the sixteen-year age difference between us. It was never an issue in *my* mind, then or now. First of all, Erwin and I were both adults when we started dating. Age was far less of a problem than the fact that we had different backgrounds, life experiences, and personalities, issues most new couples face. I'm American and he's German. That's the biggest difference of all.

The world might view Erwin as Tina's "younger man," but the truth is that, at heart, he's really sixty and I'm sixteen. Erwin has always been an old soul. He's much more mature than I am. He thinks ahead and exercises caution, while I'm the one most likely to leap without looking. He can be very set in his ways. He still plays his accordion, as he did when he was a boy. And when we first got together, I was surprised to see that he had a routine of closing doors and turning off lights before we went to bed, something I've never done. When I asked, "Why are we doing that?" "It's nighttime—we close the doors and turn off the lights," he answered, matter-of-factly. I teased him that he sounded like an old man!

Actually, I found that most people were happy for me, and even celebrated our relationship. My behavior helped older women to feel less self-conscious about becoming romantically involved with younger men. I was so confident about us, I tried not to pay attention to anything negative. Why should I? I'd already had a hard life, a bad marriage, and all that. It was time for me to take care of *me*.

My attitude about Erwin is an extension of my feelings about aging in general. I don't believe in limits. I don't care that I'm getting older, as long as I feel good and keep myself fresh and up-to-date with the times. As Deepak Chopra says, there's a new kind of "old age." We're living longer, doing more, even dressing differently. I'm not trying to dress like the young girls. I've found that I can look just as good without showing too much cleavage, or wearing very short skirts. I have to cover up a little as I get older, but there's nothing wrong with that. You just have to accept it and find a style that works for you. There's an expression, "You'll never get out of this world alive." It's true. We won't. Go forward. Do your best with your makeup, hair, and clothes. You have to *evolve*. Like Erwin, I never think of age or color as being obstacles.

Cher and I discussed this subject with Oprah during an interview a few years ago. When Cher was asked how she felt about getting older, she answered, "I think it sucks!" I disagreed. "I welcome it with open arms," I told the surprised audience, enumerating the many ways life improves with age. I explained that my senior life is so much better than when I was young—the wisdom, the way I think, my attitude. There's a good change when you're still healthy and you still look good. I will accept eighty, ninety, whatever, when it comes.

Meanwhile, when I was forty-six, I didn't look older than thirty-year-old Erwin, and I don't look older than him today. Oprah once asked if when we're alone together I ever think about the fact that Erwin's a younger man. I told her no. It just feels like me and Erwin. Even at night, there's nothing that makes me feel like I have to work at looking pretty in bed. We're past that. What's love got to do with it? A lot! We're comfortable in our own skin and, more importantly, comfortable with each other.

———

So I made the right decision when, head-over-heels in love, I packed my bags and headed for Erwin's apartment in Marienburg, Germany, a Bel Air–like suburb outside of Cologne. His place struck me as being minimalist, but I thought it was because he'd moved in recently. When I got to know Erwin a little better, I learned that "minimalist" is his middle name: he hates *stuff*. Me, I'll cover every surface with books, candles, photographs, potpourri, anything to add personality. But Erwin's philosophy is "less is more." His dream coffee table would have nothing on it but a lone television remote. More about this later . . .

Erwin's two-room apartment was a classic bachelor flat, outfitted with a great sound system, but not much else. Artwork leaned against the walls and piles of record albums were stacked everywhere, although Erwin claimed that he'd sold thousands before he moved and kept a mere few hundred of his all-time favorites. I immediately thought, *Well, this room really needs decorating.* I didn't say anything, and I didn't know when it would happen, but I already had some ideas and I couldn't wait to start the makeover.

A more pressing problem was my luggage. I planned on staying an entire month, so I'd packed about ten Louis Vuitton suitcases with a broad selection of clothing, enough to cover every possible occasion. There was no room for any of it in Erwin's one-hundred-square-meter apartment. I had to store my bags in the basement and run down to get my clothes. Erwin's neighbors had to push past the stack of "Louis" whenever they needed to use the building's washer and dryer. It was a bit of an inconvenience, but imagine their surprise when they walked into the laundry room and came across Tina Turner, rummaging through her luggage, trying to find something to wear.

My security people were with me on this trip. Strange as it seemed to me, now that I'd become an "overnight sensation," I couldn't travel without them. They slept in a nearby hotel (where they didn't have to store their bags in the basement), while I stayed with Erwin. Not that I was uncomfortable. I loved being with him. I wanted to spend *more* time together, not run away, which was how I'd always felt when I was with Ike. For the first time, I felt that I was truly in a relationship. *This is how it's supposed to be*, I told myself. We were two people, happily sharing a space, enjoying daily life.

I'm sure that Erwin rolled his eyes from time to time, as he's never impressed by celebrity and all that goes with it, not after all his years in the music business. "Stay grounded," he said. "Don't depend on the privileges that come with being famous because they can disappear as quickly as they came." It was good advice, but even *he* had to admit that it came in handy to have my security team around. We communicated via walkie-talkie. They protected me when we were out in public and made it possible for us to enjoy private time together at home. When we didn't have the energy to leave the apartment, they'd drop off food so we could have the luxury of dining alone.

I confess that there was one instance when my enthusiasm for our new life got me into the kind of trouble you'd see on an episode of *I Love Lucy*. Not all of my crazy schemes turned out to be good ideas. Erwin had to fly off to Brazil on a short business trip—just for a weekend—and I stayed in the apartment. I couldn't help myself, so, as soon he left, and I was alone, my urge to redecorate swept over me. Without a moment's hesitation, I raced over to Pesch, the famous home interiors store in Cologne, and did a whirlwind shop. Normally, fine furniture has to be ordered six months in advance. But when I pleaded for a speedy delivery, the store managed to schedule it for the very next day—one of those privileges Erwin warned against. I rearranged everything in the apartment and eagerly awaited the unveiling of his big surprise.

Erwin had a terrible trip home from Brazil—he was injured on the flight when a food cart ran over his foot—so he hobbled in on Sunday, overcome with pain. What he saw did not make him feel better. He thought he was in the wrong apartment—no, the wrong *world*, as he put it. Everywhere he looked, there was stuff, stuff, and more stuff. I'd filled the rooms with furniture and accessories. I even had someone come in to rewire his beloved sound system. I was proud as can be that I'd managed to do everything in two short days, but poor Erwin was horrified. He wished he could make everything go back to the way it was before I meddled. The situation was turning into one of my worst "Operation Oops!"

Luckily, a friend joined us for dinner that night, so Erwin had to contain his aggravation. By the next day, he'd calmed down a little and was getting used to the changes. Eventually, he accepted them. Isn't it funny that he had a harder time adjusting to new furniture than to the new woman in his life? We survived that battle, but the decorating war continues to this day. Erwin still longs for that minimalist room with a bare table and a lone remote control, while I surround myself with antiques, art, mementos—and anything and everything I consider beautiful.

Gradually, we settled into our own version of a routine, if you consider flying from one continent to another on a day off a routine. I introduced Erwin to my family during the Christmas holiday, and he passed that test with flying colors. Muh, who could be difficult, loved that he was so polite and respectful, so genuinely interested in her and in Alline. Erwin asked a lot of questions and Muh and Alline liked to talk, so it was a good mix. I wasn't surprised that they got along so well. How could my mother and sister resist Erwin's many charms? He liked them, too, and appreciated that they were so down-to-earth.

Erwin never came out and asked me to be his girlfriend, although he did ask in his charming German way, "Are we together?" Which means "Are we a couple?" It wasn't the way we would have said it in America, but I liked it. He was starting to really feel something for me, but he was afraid to move too quickly because he kept thinking, *Oh, those wild and unpredictable California girls*, remembering the naughty pass I had made at him when we first met. He worried that I was just playing, that I might run off one day. He had to learn to trust me the way I trusted him. I had no fears. I wasn't looking for a husband, I wanted to be loved. Childhood—never loved. Past relationships—never loved. My whole life—never really loved. More than anything, I needed to feel that Erwin loved me.

When work took me away, we got really good at maintaining our long-distance romance. But it was difficult to be parted by an ocean so much of the time. It meant being uprooted a lot. I explained to Erwin that I had to have a home, a place to roost. I wasn't ready to move to Germany, because I couldn't speak the language, but I decided that London would be a good choice for an intermediate step. I'd be closer to Erwin, and the city was already a second home to me. In 1988, Rhonda helped me to pack up my house in California, and I moved to Kensington, near Notting Hill.

When I first settled in London, Erwin (who was still living in Germany) flew over to spend weekends with me when I was in town. I lived in a beautiful white town house, the kind of building that I'd found so charming on my first trip to London in the sixties. I often thought about my younger self, a girl who had wished she could stay in the fairy-tale land of double-decker busses, Big Ben, and "God Save the Queen." Twenty years later, here I was, living my dream. Most of the time, I could walk the streets undisturbed. If my English fans approached me, they did it politely and discreetly, so I had a bit more freedom to move around—and enjoyed more of a private life—than I did in other cities.

Take Milan, for example. I've been chased all the way to my hotel by people waving cameras—after all, the word "paparazzi" originated in Italy. Whenever I walked out onto the street, I'd have to stop and give the fans an autograph session before I could do anything else. I loved that the Italians were so enthusiastic, but it made it a little trickier to navigate the business of everyday life.

Everywhere I went in Europe, I was astonished by the outpouring of love and support from my fans. Germany is one of my favorite countries for that reason. I never lost my audience there, even after I left the Ike and Tina Revue, and before the success of *Private Dancer*. One of my most exciting shows took place in Munich in 1985, when I was greeted by a fantastic crowd of twelve thousand loud and appreciative fans at Olympiahalle.

That night held a special meaning for me because it brought me back to the first time Ike and I played Munich. For some reason, no one had shown up at that concert—it was a sad turnout of about a hundred people. Ike was so disappointed and angry that he refused to go onstage. I had to convince him that whoever was out there deserved our best show, and he finally agreed to let us perform. To return to Munich on my own, and to see the thousands of people who came to see *me*—well, nobody can know how happy I felt. We had a wonderful time together, and the evening ended with a spectacular fireworks display.

I was touched by the reaction of my fans in Sweden when I had to cancel a concert at the last minute. I had developed a nasty sinus infection and was too sick to perform the night of the show. The promoter walked out on stage to deliver the bad news, expecting to face an angry crowd. Instead, the people were so concerned about my health that they clapped and cheered to show their support. They sent cards, letters, and flowers, and when we rescheduled, the audience was even larger than the first time. Wherever I travel in the world, I find that my fans are the best people.

Touring became a way of life for me. The *Private Dancer* tour was followed by the *Break Every Rule* tour in 1987, the *Foreign Affair* tour in 1990, and the *What's Love Got to Do with It* tour in 1993. With imagination, resources, and a wonderful family of musicians, dancers, and crew, the shows got more and more spectacular, and I loved that. At the same time, it was important to me to keep it personal. I wanted my fans to have the best possible "Tina" experience.

I did make one mistake at the beginning of the *Break Every Rule* tour. I didn't perform "Proud Mary" at the first two shows. I was a little tired of singing it, and I thought the audience might be a little tired of hearing it. It wasn't until I put the song back on the set list in Amsterdam that I realized how much we all had missed it! The crowd went crazy and sang the song for us. "We've got to bring 'Mary' back," I told my associates. "She's still rolling on the river!" On every tour, whenever we performed "Proud Mary" onstage, the entire backstage crew would drop what they were doing and dance along with us, complete with all the spins, hand motions, and head pops. This is the way we do "Proud Mary."

How did I pick my songs? It didn't have to be a song I could relate to in terms of experience. In fact, I never liked autobiographical songs because I'd done enough of those, and I sometimes got tired of singing the blues. I had to like the lyrics, but the melody was also very important to me because that's what motivates me to get into the delivery. I like songs that can go both ways and appeal to the young and the old.

The order of the songs, or the "set list," as it's called, is important, too. I always started the show with a song that would get people excited, something like "Steamy Windows," a little naughty, but also lively and fun. After a couple of songs, I'd change my clothes and start a different set, maybe with something more moody, like "Let's Stay Together." One song led to the next, until the last, explosive set of "Proud Mary" and "Nutbush," the numbers that took me out to the people. The music was organized in such a way to give the audience an emotional experience.

I'm often asked, "What was going through your head before you stepped out on the stage? What was your routine?" Here's what was happening behind the curtain. For me, the show began in my dressing room, where I mentally prepared to become "Tina." There's the everyday Tina who gets up, eats breakfast, reads, shops, and relaxes with friends. And then there's the performance side of me, the Tina who engages with the audience when all eyes are on her. It's like having two personalities. They're similar, but I definitely wanted to have a larger presence onstage.

I never did vocal exercises when getting ready for a show, although I know some singers find them helpful: I remember Mick vocalized and moved around a bit before he went on. But I was never told to do that when I first became a singer, and my body got used to working without a warm-up. I attribute my strong voice to the fact that we didn't have a telephone when I was a child. Instead, we shouted to our relatives who lived across the way, so I learned to be loud to make myself heard!

Alone in my dressing room, I always began my transformation the same way. First, I'd sit down in front of the mirror and start applying my makeup. I preferred to do it myself because professional artists can make you look too perfect, or if they're not skilled, they can make you look like a clown. I put it on slowly and sparingly—never too much. That was something I believed in even during the "Ike and Tina" days, when I had to get dressed on the bus, or in a storeroom. I liked to keep it subtle. I finished the look with a bright red lipstick, which is all you really need, because the lips are so visible. Then I put on my wig, pinning it on really tight, so there was no chance of it slipping or, God forbid, coming off.

I remember when I was with Ike, a journalist reached out to ask if she could be an Ikette for a night. She was writing an article and figured it would only take a few days to master the whole routine—dancing, singing, wearing the wig, the dress, and the shoes—and perform it onstage. I don't think she realized how much preparation was involved, how hard we worked, or that we actually had talent. The problem wasn't that she was white—we'd had white Ikettes before—or that she had an attitude (by showtime, my dancers were beyond frustrated with her). The bigger issue was that there wasn't a muscle in her body that could dance! When the show started, she lasted about thirty seconds before her wig started to slip off her head, she tripped on her own two feet, and she ended up on the floor in an Al Jolson pose straight out of "Mammy," which was a little embarrassing. The look she got from Ike was priceless. The language that followed was unrepeatable. That was the last we saw of her.

My preparation left no room for a slipped wig or wardrobe malfunction. While I was getting ready, I was constantly asking myself questions. *How do I look? Is the hair right? Do I have all the gear I need to protect me?* I had to make sure that my boobs weren't jumping around, or spilling out. Then, I had to think about my bottom. If my dress came up (or if Mick Jagger was around to pull off my skirt), was I covered properly?

Looking sexy onstage was never my primary goal, and I didn't worry about how guys would react to my look. I always played to the *women* in the audience, because if you've got the girls on your side, you've got the guys. I wanted the women to like me, so I set out to convince them that I was just having fun, not trying to steal their men.

In fact, most of the costumes that people considered sexy were practical choices. Fishnet stockings didn't run as often as the other kind. Short dresses were easier for dancing because they left my legs free, and looked good with my short torso. Leather didn't show perspiration or dirt, and it never wrinkled. So much for sex appeal.

When I finished my checklist, I'd look in the mirror one last time. If I'd done my job correctly, the woman who walked into the dressing room was gone, replaced by Tina Turner the performer. I was ready for the show.

I always held the arm of my security guard on the way to the stage. Call me superstitious, but I didn't want to twist my foot, or slip on the floor, before the show even started. The atmosphere backstage was usually very festive—we were a big family. The musicians were playing their instruments, grooving on something and dancing to get in the mood. I rarely joined them, except every now and then when they were doing a song I really liked. My dancers used to hold hands and say a prayer together, and I gently patted their backs and walked past them to the stage. I did my meditations daily, so I didn't feel the need to do anything right before the show. These moments were the calm before the storm for me. I stood in my place on the lift and waited. As soon as I heard the opening music and the spotlight found me, I was *on*, smiling at the people.

Yes, it's acting, but I mean that in a good way. You have to be someone large onstage, not who you are in your everyday life. When I was performing, I believed that every song told a story, which I expressed through singing and movement. My audience wanted theater, and that's what we gave them. You start out not knowing who they are, or how active they will be, but you want to impress them. If they were quiet and they didn't move, then we had to work together, me, the girls, and the band, to pull them in and show them how to have a good time. I'd give the girls a secret signal, as if to say, it's one of *those* audiences, and we'd *really* work.

I remember once when I stopped and said, "Hi, everybody. Oh, it's quiet in here." And then I started the show. In no time, they were on their feet and totally into it. Some audiences have a "let's see" attitude. They come in thinking *Is this show all they say it is?* and you just have to take a different approach to get them up to speed. But we always won them over in the end. I wanted them to have the best time they possibly could, and I wouldn't settle for anything less. One of my greatest pleasures was enjoying the crowd as much as they were enjoying me. You dance differently if you're having a good time. They motivated me. I'd give a little wave of my hand, and if they all waved back, I knew they were focused.

I had a special relationship with my dancers. Sometimes, I looked at their lovely faces and thought of them as a wonderful bouquet of flowers. But they were never decorative. We really worked hard on that stage, and every move was calculated. We planned our routine so the dancers did most of the traveling onstage, while I concentrated on the singing. If I stopped singing for an instrumental solo, they'd come over to me and I'd dance with them, until I picked up the song again. The moves looked easy and effortless, but they were carefully choreographed. In fact, the girls were so used to following my lead that, one night, I fell down in the middle of a song and they all followed me to the floor! They thought it was some new choreography I had improvised on the spot.

Another time, my foot caught on something and I went flop. I looked at my saxophone player to lift me up, but he just kept playing. He probably thought I was acting when I said, "Timmy! Help me out!" Clare, my head dancer, thought the same thing. She saw me, totally flat out, but she figured I knew what I was doing because I always did! With no help from them, I jumped up and just kept dancing.

I think people wonder why I didn't fall more often. "How did you dance in those high, high heels?" they want to know. Let's talk about the heels. I got used to wearing them after so many years of dancing onstage, but I did have a method. You always stay a little bit on your toes, with your weight thrust forward, and try not to stand flat on your feet. Toes are surprisingly strong. One night, I was dancing on a stage that turned out to be slightly tilted and I felt myself falling forward. I was saved by my ten little toes: I was amazed that they gripped through my shoes and held me in place.

I love wearing beautiful shoes onstage . . . Louboutins, Manolo Blahniks—my wall of shoes is a tribute to my favorite designers. But one of my secret weapons for endurance was Pasquale Fabrizio, a master shoemaker who reminded me of Geppetto from *Pinocchio*. Cher told me about him. Although he was located in Los Angeles, Pasquale and his workers, who sat on itty-bitty stools at little tables, looked just like old-fashioned cobblers in European fairy tales. They made extraordinary shoes for everyone in show business, from Frank Sinatra to Liza Minnelli. Pasquale built a model of the client's foot, which is called a "last," and used it to handcraft specialty shoes, reinforcing the heel and sole with a metal shank, so it couldn't break. You can't dance in a loose shoe, and Pasquale's creations fit so beautifully that they felt like an extension of the leg. I could stand, dance, do anything, for long periods of time, without worrying that my feet would fail me.

I really needed my feet the night I appeared at the Maracanã Stadium in Brazil in 1988. Incredibly, over 180,000 people showed up for my *Break Every Rule* concert. I had often fantasized about what it would be like to entertain a really big audience, but I never imagined an audience *that* big, as in "Guinness World Record for number of concert tickets sold by a solo performer" *big*. I couldn't really see individuals—the crowd was massive and stretched back into darkness—but I'm told that there were more women than men, and fans of all ages, from teens to grandparents. They were so happy and excited to be there. The one thing I didn't foresee was how much work it would be to sing and dance in front of that number of people. I never asked Mick, and I probably should have, "How do you perform for such an enormous audience?" You feel like you need to be everywhere on the stage simultaneously, running back and forth to make sure that you get to everyone. That night, I moved around so much in the record-breaking heat and humidity that I probably lost six pounds just by sweating, and that was while I was wearing a succession of miniskirts.

Later, I discovered that there's an art to entertaining tens of thousands of people. I learned to alternate my position on the stage: I'd sing a certain song facing one side of the arena, move to the middle for the next song, and then switch to the other side for the next. I worked different parts of the house at different times, making sure that everyone got to see something aimed at them by the end of the show. That's why I started using screens. I know some singers don't care for them because they believe a concert should be a real-life experience. But how do you have an impact on fans in a large stadium, when they could be sitting almost a mile away from the stage? I think about those people way out there. I want them to see what I'm doing—my facial expressions when I'm singing, and the details of my choreography—so they can experience my performance just like the fans in the front rows, and leave with the feeling that they have seen something spectacular.

My wildest dream was to have this kind of success—to pack a stadium, to walk out on a stage and look at the crowd, knowing that they came to see me. What a wonderful turn my life had taken. After so much unhappiness, after thinking that love of any kind would never be a part of my story, love was all around me. I enjoyed the warm embrace of my audience at every concert; I had a wonderful relationship with Erwin; and, after the publication of my autobiography, *I, Tina*, in 1986 (and the subsequent film adaptation, *What's Love Got to Do with*

It, in 1993), I was overwhelmed by love, support, and gratitude from women—and men—who heard my story and were inspired by it.

I could not have been more surprised. For years, I was reluctant to talk about my experiences with Ike for obvious, and sometimes less obvious, reasons. I was so embarrassed when people heard the horrible details. I didn't want an ugly life, and I got myself trapped into one. Then I had to talk about it, and talk about it, and talk about it. I couldn't begin to answer the questions people asked once they knew what had happened between us. They were so personal. "Why did you stay? Why did you leave? Why didn't you say anything at the time? Can you show me your scars?" I couldn't explain it to myself, how could I make anyone else understand? It was all so complicated that it took decades for me to move beyond the pain and confusion.

I found the subject so upsetting that I could never bring myself to watch *What's Love Got to Do with It*. And when I did see a few clips on television, I wasn't happy with some of the choices the filmmakers made—for example, the way they dressed us was very "zoot suit," and by that I mean exaggerated, even tasteless. They got the house wrong, too, although they filmed in the actual house where we lived. Somehow, they made us seem like a different kind of people. Creative differences aside, I didn't want to spend two hours reliving the nightmare I'd spent years trying so hard to forget.

Whatever I felt about Ike and our past, and as much as I wanted to put it behind me, I was moved that my sad story had the power to help others. Oprah, who has interviewed me many times, had a habit of asking me the same tough question: "Do you remember the first time Ike hit you?" Sensing that I was tired of reliving these memories, she said privately, "Tina, you know why I keep asking." Oprah saw a higher purpose in our discussion. She helped me understand how important it was for me to keep talking, that I was offering a lesson. It was an opportunity to reach out to abused women and bring the difficult subject into the light. If they heard me talking honestly about *my* experiences, they might find the courage to do something about their own situations.

I'm told over and over again by fans, those who approach me in person, others who write very emotional letters, that some aspect of my story—my escape from Ike, my determination to survive on my own, my dedication, my resilience, and yes, my optimism—actually did help them. Whenever we were on tour, Roger and I couldn't walk through an airport without being stopped by someone who wanted to share a story with me. Usually, I was approached by women, but I remember a man yelling, "Tina Turner—I saw your movie and I will never beat my wife again," a disturbing message, but a positive one in the end.

Oprah sat next to a woman at one of my *Wildest Dreams* concerts who confided, "I came because I was looking for the courage to leave the man who beats me. Tonight, I found that courage." Oprah told me, "You don't just dance and sing. You represent possibility. When people see you performing, they know you've come up from the depths of despair. It means that however down a woman is, she can be like you."

David Bowie used to call me a "phoenix rising from the ashes." I know it sounds corny, but when he said it, it was pure poetry, and his words truly expressed the feelings I had inside. For anyone who's in an abusive relationship, I say this: nothing can be worse than where you are now. If you get up and leave, if you rise from the ashes, life will open up for you. But you have to do it your way. You know, I've lived my life the only way I knew how, and good has come of it. I never imagined having an impact on anyone else, but I'm happy that a life such as mine can be an inspiration to others.

9

"TOTAL CONTROL"

"I would sell my soul for total control"

Peter Lindbergh, who is a truly great photographer, took one of my favorite pictures when we were shooting the cover of my 1989 *Foreign Affair* album in Paris. We were on the Eiffel Tower, and Peter asked if I would mind posing closer to the edge. I can do better than that, I thought. After all, I was the little girl who liked to climb trees. I still liked adventure, and I *loved* making anything—even a photograph—more exciting for the people. Why stand still on the Eiffel Tower when I could climb?

I was wearing a short dress designed by the late Azzedine Alaïa, who was a dear friend of mine. I loved his clothes—you become very French as soon as you put them on. When I proposed doing something a little extreme, I think I made Peter a bit nervous—he looked at my high-heeled feet and said, "With the shoes?" As for Roger, he was ready to have a heart attack. *"Don't do it in case you fall, the insurance will never cover it,"* he managed to spit out as quickly as he could, hoping to stop me. But I ignored him and scrambled up the side. I planted my weight on my heels, held on with one arm, tossed my hair, and arched my back, with the glorious City of Lights in the background. That's how I wanted to live my life, with Europe at my feet. With every passing year, I felt increasingly at home in the Old World, and I knew I wanted to make it my new world.

There were many reasons why I was considering a permanent move to Europe. For one thing (and this may have been subliminal),

I felt safe abroad because there was no chance of running into Ike, or seeing reminders of our life together. When I was inducted into the Rock & Roll Hall of Fame in 1991, at a ceremony at the Waldorf Astoria in New York, someone handed me a program to sign and I was shocked to see Ike's signature on it—then I looked across the room and there he was. We didn't come face-to-face that day, or any other day, as it turns out, but our near encounter reminded me how nice it was to be in a place where I didn't have to worry about him coming around every corner. I could forget about him in a foreign country.

As my career unfolded, I also felt that I was experiencing my greatest success abroad. The energy was different in America, where everything was about getting a hit record. Yet some records were held back because they were considered too black to be white, or too white to be black, or something silly like that. There seemed to be less discrimination in Europe. My audience there was growing fast, my fans were extremely loyal, and there were so many artists, writers, and producers who wanted to work with me.

But, if I'm being completely honest, I'll say that falling in love with a wonderful European man was the best reason of all to move there. Eventually, it made sense for me to move to Germany, so Erwin and I could have a real home together. Cologne already felt like home because I had spent so much time there with Erwin. In 1990, we found a stately brick house and did a major renovation that took several months to complete. And, because a house in one beautiful European city is never enough—a crazy concept for someone who was usually on the road—I also fell in love with a villa in the South of France. A psychic once told me that I would get a house surrounded by flowers, and that turned out to be my house high atop the mountains overlooking Nice. I called it "Anna Fleur" because of the flowers and as a sweet reminder of my real name, Anna. My passion for decorating peaked in this classic villa, where my imagination went wild. I combined museum-quality Louis Philippe–period pieces with furniture that was Art Deco, contemporary French, and anything else that spoke to me—and somehow, as I'd known it would, it all worked! I set aside a special room for meditation on the second floor, and that's where I began most days. I spent several years turning the house into the refuge of my dreams.

Mike Wallace came to "Anna Fleur" to interview me for the show *60 Minutes*. We had such a good time together, talking candidly and walking through the house and gardens. At one point, he looked around and asked if I thought I deserved all this luxury. "I deserve more," I answered without hesitation. I'd been working for almost forty years, and I'd earned every dollar the hard way. Whether I was enjoying the emotional satisfaction of being with the man I loved, or the bounty that came with career success, I was both appreciative and proud of what I had accomplished. And I knew I deserved it.

My friends Bono and Edge of U2 had homes in the nearby town of Eze-sur-Mer, just outside of Nice. One night, I was invited over for dinner, and as I was walking up the driveway I heard an unmistakable voice commenting on *my* unmistakable voice—it was Jack Nicholson drawling, "I hear you coming." Even though we had both starred in the movie *Tommy*, we never shot at the same time, so this was our first meeting. We spent the whole evening talking, trading stories about our experiences—my singing, his acting, our feelings about performing. At some point, Bono and The Edge mentioned that they were writing the theme song for the new James Bond movie, *GoldenEye*, and they wanted me to sing it.

I was thrilled . . . until I heard Bono's demo, which was strange little snippets of music that didn't add up to a real melody. *What is this?* I thought. I didn't even know what key to sing it in. Bono said that after he sent it, he realized it was really bad, so we could laugh about that. But I told myself to just step into the shoes and learn it. I absorbed it and sang it the way I would do it, and even Bono was impressed. I think we recorded it in two or three takes. After that, I actually liked the way "GoldenEye" transformed my singing. I had never done a song like that, and it really gave me a chance to be creative in terms of taking these rough fragments and turning them into a smooth and expressive song that worked for the movie and became a real showstopper whenever I performed it on tour.

The "GoldenEye" music video was pure glamour. My hair was swept up in my version of a classic chignon. I wore a form-fitting, off-the-shoulder white evening gown with a graceful slit that framed my legs whenever I moved. And for the final touch—I added long, glittering diamond earrings. The look was a wonderful combination of retro Shirley Bassey "Goldfinger" and modern Bond, and I think the song worked beautifully with this striking visual.

While I was happy in the many places Erwin and I called home during our first decade together, I experienced a new level of contentment when, in 1995, destiny brought us to Switzerland. I say "destiny," but the reason behind our move was more prosaic than poetic. Erwin was asked to move to Zurich to run EMI's office there, and like a good *Frau*, I was accompanying my partner to his new location. We rented a house while we looked at real estate, and then one day, we drove through the gates of the Château Algonquin. I got out of the car, looked up, and felt chills all over my body, the same feeling that overwhelmed me when I met Erwin. This time, I experienced love at first sight with a house—my dream house. The old-fashioned villa, located on Lake Zurich, suffered from neglect and was in bad shape, but I could see that its flaws were cosmetic. I knew instantly what I would do to make it beautiful, and I couldn't wait to get started. "I lived the first half of my life in America. The second half I'll live in Europe," I told *Harper's Bazaar*. Finally, I was home.

What did I like about Switzerland? Everything! Switzerland is not Tennessee, but I'm always reminded of the landscapes I enjoyed when I was growing up, especially when I see the farms and meadows in the Swiss countryside. I love exploring the cities, with their beautifully maintained historic buildings. And everywhere I go, I'm struck by how clean the country is. The air is so fresh that the simple act of breathing feels like drinking a cold, clear glass of water.

I also like the way the seasons change—each one is distinct. The trees lose their leaves, then they come back the following year. It sounds simple—I took it for granted when I was a child. But we've lost that sense of nature's rhythm in so many parts of the world. Here, there's a real winter—cold, crisp, and picturesque, with storybook snow. We have an old-fashioned ice-skating rink in our town that looks like a scene on a picture postcard.

Switzerland is famous for its scenery, but the country has other attributes that appeal to me. I like the government here—in Switzerland, a law is a law. "No Speeding" means exactly that. Break the law by driving too fast, and your license will be taken away. Rules are not ambiguous, so you always know where you stand. Oh, and *everyone* in Switzerland is punctual, which is something I had to work at in the beginning. When I first moved here, and arrived "fashionably late" at a function, someone gently chided me for being tardy, saying that I couldn't be late just because I was a celebrity. I didn't need to be told twice.

In this country, courtesy always comes first. At the supermarket, the gas station, everywhere, before any business can be conducted, people are expected to greet each other with a pleasant "Good morning," or a "Good afternoon"—to connect, human being to human being. In America, we tend to be in a hurry, so we often forget about the little niceties, or dismiss them as being superficial. Once, when I heard the doorbell ring, I shouted to Erwin without thinking, "Answer the door!" He was so offended. I should have said, "Darling, would you please answer the door?" Which is exactly how I would say it the next time the bell rang. Being polite and considerate, in speech and in actions, really improves the quality of life for everyone.

Lucky for me, the Swiss have a long-standing tradition of welcoming foreigners. Erwin and I have made wonderful friends over the years, and there is nothing "show business" about our circle, or any other aspect of our life at the Château Algonquin. The bottom line is that I have always felt comfortable, safe, and happy in Switzerland.

By the late 1990s, it made sense to bring my family, meaning my sons, my mother, and my sister, to Europe whenever we wanted to spend time together. But these reunions were not always easy. No matter how old and experienced we are, or how confident and successful we may become, there's always a part of us that wonders, *What does my mother think of me?* I could pretend in my matter-of-fact way that I wasn't bothered by my mother's abandonment when I was young, or that I wasn't frustrated by her denial of my talent when I was with Ike, but her indifference hurt. I didn't let it affect my behavior toward her, that was never my nature. Still, I knew who she was and what her limitations were. I went through my life with the knowledge that she didn't love me the way a mother is supposed to love her child.

When Ike entered our lives, Muh viewed him as the sun, the moon, and the stars. In her mind, he was the celebrity, the master-mind behind whatever money we made, or success we achieved. She just couldn't see his faults, even when his bad behavior was taking place right before her eyes. She certainly didn't think that I was the source of any of our good fortune. According to her, I should have been grateful that Ike kept me around. When I tried to run away, Muh was the one who helped Ike find me. She always took his side. After all, he owned the house where she lived, so that bought him her loyalty. Muh even maintained her relationship with Ike after we divorced. She still called him her son-in-law. I didn't want to hear any of the details, but I knew they stayed in touch.

Muh was "Team Ike" until my success was too big for her to ig-nore. Then, she really went on that Tina Turner trip because, more than anything, she loved being the mother of a celebrity. If we went out together, she had to sit at the front table so everyone could see she was with Tina. I wished she had expressed that kind of love for Anna Mae.

She was my mother, and I had the means to take care of her, so I did. Over the years, I moved her from St. Louis to California, where I bought her a house. She didn't like it, so I bought her another and filled it with furniture. She wanted to work, so I arranged a little job at a beauty salon, where she could interact with people. I listened to her endless complaints. When I visited her in Los Angeles, I scrubbed her kitchen if it was dirty. I fixed whatever mistakes she made, and some of them were whoppers—like the time she blew out the entire air-

---

conditioning system in the new house I had just purchased for her. I brought her to my homes in England, France, and Switzerland to show her my world, and invited her to enjoy my success.

None of it mattered to Muh. Somehow, she still doubted that I was capable of accomplishing anything. When Erwin came into my life, she decided that he must be the one responsible for the beautiful décor of our homes, which showed how little she knew about *me* or *him*. I don't know how Erwin kept a straight face when he calmly tried to explain to her that "Tina is the interior decorator." As if Erwin would dream of decorating anything!

Hostilities mounted one time when Muh and my sister Alline came to visit us in the South of France. At this point Muh was ill. She was a difficult patient and had been through at least twenty nurses. Now she wanted Alline to take care of her all the time, but she wasn't very nice to her, and I felt sorry for my sister. There was always something that compelled Muh to complain, or to pick a fight. I desperately wanted peace for all of us. I wanted to get up in the morning, enjoy the beautiful view of the Mediterranean, and be happy. I suggested to Muh that she should stop creating such havoc in the family. "You read the Bible and you say it's supposed to help you, but it's not helping if you're fighting with Alline all the time," I told her.

Well, that's all I had to say. She was ready to come back at me twice as hard, but this time, I decided to take control of our broken mother-daughter situation, once and for all. "Muh," I said firmly, "there's no room for argument. Either you make peace with Alline, and change your attitude, or I will arrange for someone to take you home to California. You can't stay here like this." Somehow, my words got through to her. She understood that I meant what I said, and realized that she had to straighten up and fly right, or else. After that, there were no more complaints.

My mother passed away in 1999.

I was deeply affected by her death, in part because I mourned the relationship we should have had with each other but never did. I thought about it, and chose not to go to her church service, because I believed my mother should be the center of attention that day. My decision generated some nasty press about how full of myself I must have been to skip my mother's service. Of course, that wasn't the case. I didn't want the occasion to be all about me, with photographers and fans giving me all the attention and ignoring Muh.

I can't say the same about Ike. My sister told me that he came to the house and offered to drive my family to the church, but Alline told him they already had a ride. It bothered me that he was named in one of the memorials as Muh's "cherished son-in-law." His presence that day generated the worst kind of "Ike and Tina" tabloid headlines, the ones I had hoped to avoid.

Shortly after the service, I quietly flew in for a private funeral. My mother was cremated, and I arranged for the whole family to gather on a boat to spread her ashes to the sea off the coast of California. Needless to say, Ike was not invited.

My mother and grandmother are often in my thoughts. One day, when I was in a reading with a psychic, I felt their presence intensely. The psychic announced that there were spirits with us—that she could hear my grandmother and mother communicating (arguing, more likely) and that Mama Georgie was telling Muh, "You know you didn't treat Ann right." Trying to defend herself, my mother answered, "I tried." "Well, you didn't try hard enough," my grandmother snapped back, refusing to let her get away with it. Even in the spirit world, and presumably for all of eternity, Mama Georgie wasn't about to let Muh forget that she wasn't a proper mother to me.

Motherhood is difficult. We have certain expectations of how our parents should behave, and they often disappoint us because they're only human. I know that my children would have benefited from having a mother and father who stayed home with them. But that's not what happened. We were always on the road, and Ike's demons—his blind ambition, his drug addiction, his rage and the violence that went with it—fostered a climate of fear and uncertainty that affected the boys when they were growing up. They saw my black eyes and heard our endless fighting. Ike's children never reacted, but my oldest son, Craig, who was very sensitive and emotional, was very troubled by it. One day when Ike was lashing out at me, Craig knocked on the door and said, "Mother, are you all right?" My first thought was *Oh, this can't happen in the house.* I didn't want my children to hear or see what was going on. I knew it would make an impression on them, and it did. We were scarred in different ways by Ike's behavior.

I raised all four boys, and I wanted the best for them, but I was never a mushy mother hen type. As they got older, I told them, "I'm not going to take care of you. I want you to learn how to take care of yourselves." I truly believed that encouraging them to be self-reliant would help them more in life than anything I could give them. They've had their share of troubles. I've spent the most time with Craig, who always seems sad when our visit is over, just as he was when he was a baby. Some feelings never leave you.

Ronnie, who used to brag to the others that he was the only "real" one, the son of both Ike and Tina, has locked heads with me since he was a teenager. Like his father, he had a problem with drugs (these dependencies can be genetic), and played fast and loose with the law when he was younger. In his wild days, he was picked up by the police for having a number of unpaid parking tickets. They put him in a cell, and to his surprise, there was Ike, in the same cell, at the same time. What are the odds of that? Ike immediately saw it as an opportunity—he had Ronnie doing his chores, making his bed and cleaning up. Fortunately, Ronnie saw the experience as a wake-up call. If he didn't want to end up like his father—and he claimed that he didn't—he had to get a grip on his life. He's a musician, so he has the burden of working in the shadow of two famous parents.

Ike Jr. and Michael drifted away from me after the divorce. I won't try to tell their stories for them. But I will say that I never wanted the boys to depend on me financially, because I knew that kind of help would make them weak. "I'm not the Valley Bank," I used to joke. They have to use their own arms and legs to support themselves, just as I used mine.

In 2000, after enjoying a few years off from my intense performing schedule, I decided to go back on the road with the *Twenty Four Seven Millennium* tour. I truly envisioned this tour as being my last—a sprint through Europe and North America with a show that would give my audiences everything they'd ever wanted. My feeling was that, after forty-four years of performing, it was probably time to retire and let people remember me at my best. I was happy to do it one more time, and I was determined to make it a show to remember.

When I had started playing arenas, my shows got bigger, more conceptual, and benefited from very imaginative staging. Even though I had said I wanted to be an actress, I stopped feeling the pull to perform on screen because I felt as if I were in a movie every time I stepped out on the stage. Each show was a play, an act, a small (or not so small) movie, so to speak, with a cast (me, my dancers, and the band), an enormous crew, and stunning sets. Mark Fisher, the architectural genius who designed sets for everyone from Pink Floyd to the Rolling Stones, U2, and Lady Gaga, outdid himself with a massive production that offered breathtaking special effects.

The big stunner—and the feature that almost sent Roger to an early grave during every show—was the "Claw," a sixty- to eighty-foot, cantilevered arm that carried me out over the audience. I danced across the narrow platform on my heels—sometimes pretending to slip just a *little* to make Roger nervous—and I hung over the railing to get closer to the people—so close that I could see their faces, actually look into their eyes, and they could see me. I loved that moment of connection and togetherness.

The *Twenty Four Seven* tour was very demanding and left me longing for an extended break—maybe a permanent one. I've never been one of those people who can't relax. My work is noisy, but I'm someone who enjoys being quiet. How did I spend my time when I wasn't working? I didn't need to listen to music. I liked to read, meditate, talk to Erwin, and indulge my guiltiest of guilty pleasures by watching scary movies, the scarier the better. My years of performing shaped my daily routine in such a way that I became a confirmed night owl. To this day, Erwin and I stay up until the wee hours of the morning and then get up late. There's a large metal sign posted at the entrance of the Château Algonquin that says, "No deliveries before noon."

When we're not busy at home, one of our favorite activities is driving to our little house in the country. There's a wonderful expression for the remote part of the world where the house is located. They call it *"wo sich Fuchs und Hase gute Nacht sagen,"* which means, "where the fox and the rabbit say good night." Otherwise known as nowhere! We like it that way. Nowhere to be, nothing to do.

When we go to the country, the car is our confessional. I strongly recommend this form of travel therapy to all couples. While we drive, with Erwin at the wheel and me riding shotgun, we talk about everything. Whatever the subject, we lay it out openly, we don't color it, and nothing is off-limits. As Erwin likes to say, "There are no secrets in the cockpit." We learned this from the Dalai Lama. Not the car part . . . but the idea that confrontation is positive. "One thing," he said, "always do confrontation. When you hold something in, it works against you in the long run." Once Erwin heard that, he started to open up. Our conversations can get a little heated, and sometimes it takes time for me to cool off—I'm emotional that way. But, no matter what, we talk it through. We know there has to be compromise in a relationship, and we live by that. In a funny twist, my experiences in a bad relationship with Ike have helped me to appreciate—and maintain—my good relationship with Erwin.

The one sensitive topic after all these years? Decorating. Yes, the decorating wars are ongoing, especially in the country, and no amount of time dedicated to car therapy will ever change that. When I first started spending time at the country house, I thought, *Am I going to be comfortable here?* I convinced Erwin to go shopping, and I'd say, "Darling, do you like this?" while pointing to a particular piece of furniture. Erwin's pretend answer would be yes, and then he'd pull the plug on me and order whatever he wanted, usually the opposite of whatever I selected.

This house was Erwin's refuge, a place to keep simple and masculine. Finally, I said to myself, "Okay, Tina. You've had all these houses. Back off. This is his. Let him have it." But it was—and is—really hard!

Erwin loves to work with his hands—he owns every power tool under the sun. He's also fascinated by anything with a motor—a car, a motorcycle, even a boat—and his garage is state-of-the-art. For Erwin, driving is a sport. He goes off on weeklong road trips with his fellow car and motorcycle enthusiasts, and he's always trying to explain to me why these drives are so enjoyable. I say, "It's a ride. It's a road. It's a car. What's special about that?" But Erwin says it's a brotherhood, with the kind of deep, through-thick-and-through-thin friendships that come from having shared interests. He argues that any negative image of bikers is just wrong—that they are good, reliable people. All I know is that he's likely to return from these trips smelling like gasoline. And there was that time he came home from the "Mille Miglia" race in Italy with a little problem. The car, a red Ferrari 340 America racing car from 1951, had a heating issue—the exhaust had made the floor of the car so hot that the rubber sole of Erwin's Timberland shoe melted off. He had to wrap it with gaffer's tape so he could walk. That's dedication! I tease him, but I love that Erwin is passionate about his interests.

My life became so quiet during this period that it might have been the time when the question "Did Tina Turner die?" started to trend in Google searches. If there was any doubt as to whether I was dead or alive, all rumors were put to rest in 2005, when I was honored at the Kennedy Center in Washington, D.C. I resisted it at first, because I couldn't imagine that I had done anything to deserve a medal—I always saw myself as someone who just got up and went to work. But

I dressed up in my best Galliano, joined my fellow honorees, Robert Redford, Tony Bennett, Julie Harris, and Suzanne Farrell, and listened to people say incredibly nice things about me, including President George W. Bush, who announced that I had the most famous legs in show business.

I sat in the theater, watching Al Green, Queen Latifah, and Melissa Etheridge perform my signature songs, and they were all wonderful in their own way. But the real revelation that evening was Beyoncé. She stepped out on the stage wearing one of the first dresses Bob Mackie designed for me (he actually had a duplicate in his archives) and said, "Every now and then, when I think of inspiration, I think of the two Tinas in my life—that's my mother, Tina, and of course, the amazing Tina Turner. I'll never forget the first time I saw you perform. I never in my life saw a woman so powerful, so fierce." I was touched by her heartfelt words. Then, she started singing "Proud Mary." I'll tell you, she did a performance that lit the place up. The audience was on their feet the entire time, moving to the music. Everybody was looking at me to see how I felt about someone else doing *my* song. I loved it! I couldn't wait to go backstage to tell Beyoncé how fierce and powerful *she* was.

I was thrilled to meet Caroline Kennedy that night—I instantly thought of her mother and how much she meant to me, and like everyone else in my generation, I had memories of Caroline and her brother when they were little kids. The old Kennedy charm still had a powerful effect on me. I leapt up and exclaimed, "I came because of you!"—every bit as enthusiastic as I had been when I spotted Jackie in that hotel lobby so many years ago. I was so happy to see Caroline, and to hear her soft voice talking about my life made everything worthwhile.

She described my singing career, and how I became a star. "But," she added, "when Tina takes the wig off, the darkness comes."

But that darkness was lifting. It was becoming such a distant memory that, in 2007, when I learned that Ike had died from a cocaine overdose, I felt strangely disconnected. I knew from the kids that Ike had a hard life. He never got up from under the drugs, he was in and out of prison, and he kept chasing that elusive hit record. His unhappiness weighed so heavily on him that, ultimately, he was destroyed by it. It was a sad story.

Of course, the press bombarded me with questions, looking for a headline and hoping I would issue some kind of statement. But I kept a silent and respectful distance. Ike was totally gone from my life. It was like hearing about a person I didn't know anymore, a person I hadn't known for almost thirty years, in fact. When I realized that I didn't feel anything, I understood that I had truly moved on.

During my break, I channeled my artistic impulses into a music project in Switzerland. My friend Regula Curti invited me to work with her on the *Beyond* project, her mission to record overlapping and interwoven Christian and Buddhist prayers, and bring them to the people. Chanting was (and is) an important part of my life, and working with Regula to record *Beyond*, four CDs in all, gave me the opportunity to express my spirituality through song. I was eager to share a spiritual message, but I wasn't sure what exactly that message should be, so I turned to Deepak Chopra for help. Erwin and I traveled to the Chopra Center in California, where we met with Deepak and asked for his advice. I came away inspired. "Start every day singing like the birds—singing takes you beyond, beyond, beyond, beyond" was one of the messages I wanted to communicate to the *Beyond* audience.

I know I said that the *Twenty Four Seven* tour would be my last—that I considered myself retired. But a few things happened to make me reconsider that decision. I had the great pleasure of performing "Proud Mary" with Beyoncé at the 2008 Grammy Awards. She's one of a kind, a strong woman with a strong voice. Singing and dancing with her took me back to the nights when I had so much fun with my dancers. Sometimes the best part of my job was me and my girls being naughty onstage, as naughty as we wanted to be. It got me thinking . . . did I miss it? Even a tiny bit?

Then one day, I was sitting next to Sophia Loren at an Armani fashion show in Milan. We started talking about what we had been up to lately, and I mentioned that I was taking a break from singing. "How long?" she asked. When I answered, "Oh, about seven years," she snapped, "Break over! People want to see you. Get back to work."

Because of my appearance on the Grammys, I found I was getting more than the usual amount of mail from fans. Wherever I went, people slipped me notes, little scraps sometimes scribbled on paper napkins. I saved all of them, and suddenly I realized I had a sizable pile. At that point, I called Roger and said, "It's time for one last tour." At the age of sixty-nine, I was ready to come out of my "retirement" and get back on the road. Fittingly, the *Fiftieth Anniversary* tour would celebrate my half century (oh, that sounds like such a long time) as a singer. We planned on starting in Missouri, where my career started with Ike and the Kings of Rhythm.

I always wanted my shows to be bigger and more exciting for the people, but when we scheduled our opening night in Kansas City, some clueless executive made the decision that I shouldn't walk out on the "Claw" when I sang "Nutbush" because it would be an insurance risk.

He probably thought I was too old to keep my balance. Roger said, "Fine, but who's going to tell Tina?" The answer was, no one—no one dared to tell Tina. I danced my heart out on that Claw, hanging over the audience and singing "Nutbush one more time!" And that was definitely one of the nights I pretended to slip!

I was excited to get back to work. But I did notice that I wasn't as energetic as I used to be. At my age, feeling tired was to be expected, considering that I was on a demanding international tour. Plus, I was living with high blood pressure. I had been diagnosed in 1978, and back then, I didn't think much of it. It was genetic—both my mother and sister had it. I don't remember being told exactly what high blood pressure was, or how it might affect my body. I took it literally, like "high" blood pressure was normal for me—so I didn't worry about getting it down to a lower number. In 1985, my doctor gave me medication, a pill to take once a day, and that was that.

Some nights, as I put on my makeup, I had to push myself to get in the mood. No matter what I was feeling in my dressing room—the lethargy, the aches and pains, the exhaustion—by the time I stepped out on that stage, I was Tina, and the audience saw the Tina they wanted to see. But I knew the difference. For me, every song I sing is an opportunity to take flight, to soar. With each show, it became harder and harder for me to get into second gear, to fly the way I was used to flying.

I believed that my body had started to react to working with high blood pressure and the medication, and that was the reason I couldn't hit my notes. Dammit! I wanted to hit those notes. Whatever was holding me back, I had to fight it, and it took every drop of energy and life for me to make it through my performance each night. Roger would come into my dressing room after the show and look at me, kind of like he knew that I was just too tired to keep this up much longer.

At one point during the tour, I got sick with a very bad chest cold. We had to reschedule a couple of shows, so our final performance was set for May 5, 2009, in Sheffield, a city in Yorkshire about three hours north of London. Sheffield was the hometown of my lead dancer, Claire, so we really had fun that night. I wanted everyone to leave that place having had the best time. I'm sure that anyone who was in the audience remembers Tina Turner's last show. I think over a million people in North America and Europe ended up seeing the *Fiftieth Anniversary* tour, and to this day, fans tell me how much they enjoyed it.

After the final performance, I went back to the hotel. I was very quiet. I knew this was it. I got up the next morning, didn't see anybody, not even Roger, and boarded the plane with Erwin. I sat there, still, calm, resolute. I took a deep breath and told myself, "I'm not going back."

Let me say this carefully, because I don't want anyone to take it the wrong way, but after working so hard for so many years, I was ready to stop. This was the moment to do it because I wanted to finish with my fans remembering me at my best. I didn't want them to come to a show in a year, or two years, and think, *Oh, she used to be good*. I had a lot of pride and I've always had great timing. There's a wise expression, "Leave the party before it's over." I was ready to say goodbye to "Proud Mary," ready to hang up my dancing shoes, and ready to go home.

10

"COMPLICATED DISASTER"

"All the plans we were making

Just got washed away with the tears"

I t's so funny when people ask, "Well, what are you going to *do* now that you're retired." The whole point is *not* to do anything— not to have to, and not to plan to. I wanted to be at home with my things. I wanted to shop for food, take walks with Erwin, work in my garden and put my hands in the soil, watch the seasons change by the lake, and most of all, I wanted to enjoy the quiet. I don't need music, although every now and then there are certain songs that make me want to sing along. I'll tell you what I like these days, "Something Just Like This" (*"doo-doo-doo, doo-doo-doo, doo-doo-doo, doo-doo-doo, doo-doo-doo, doo-doo-doo"*) by The Chainsmokers and Coldplay. I love that one!

I saw Mick at a show sometime after my final tour, and I sensed that he wanted to reprimand me when I told him I was retiring. The only time I remember him being silent and not coming back at me with a quick retort was when I asked him, "Mick, do you ever get tired?" He was quiet for a long time. I suspected the answer was yes, but he would never say that. He has his own way about him. I think he will stay out there as long as he possibly can, as long as he can walk. And that's fine. He's Mick Jagger of the Rolling Stones, and he's really, really good at it.

I loved retirement from the start. I felt good, and I think I still looked good; I certainly didn't look my age. I'm not one to exercise— my figure always came from my work, from all those years of dancing.

———

I say that the main reason I've stayed in shape is that I've spent fifty years doing the most intensive stage workouts ever! But I can also say that I've never used drugs, or smoked a cigarette, and that helps. I like to get eight hours of sleep whenever possible, and I don't just leap out of bed unless I have to be up for an appointment. I move slowly these days because I like things to be nice . . . and *easy.*

I must be doing something right because in 2013, German *Vogue* asked me to be on its cover. I think I can safely say that, at the age of seventy-three, I was the oldest cover "girl" in *Vogue*'s history. I was happy to strike a confident pose for photographers Claudia Knoepfel and Stefan Indlekofer, my hands resting on my hips and wearing a stunning blue gown by Giorgio Armani, because I felt I was making a very positive statement for women of all ages. When I was perform-ing, I used to say that age was never a priority, or even a thought. I was ageless. I feel the same way about how I live my life now. If you take care of yourself inside and out, you can radiate beauty and happiness. The number, whatever it is, doesn't mean a thing.

But with maturity, there comes a time when you have to start put-ting things in place, when you want to take control. I decided to curate my life—to get rid of anything I didn't need. I sold some property, including my house in the South of France, which was beautiful but no longer a place where I wanted to spend time because I was so happy in Switzerland. And I started thinking about Erwin. We had been to-gether for twenty-six years, a couple in every way, except legally. He was the closest person to me in this life, and I thought it was unfair that if anything happened to me he would have no say or legal stand-ing. We both knew it was time to take the next step.

I said yes to Erwin's romantic marriage proposal on our wonderful cruise through the Greek isles in 2012. I also made a commitment to our life together in Switzerland by applying for citizenship. I don't want to give the wrong impression about my decision to give up my American passport. A lot of thought went into it. I will never surrender the part of me that was born in America, or that feels "American." But my life changed when I fell in love with Erwin and started living in Europe. With every passing year, I had fewer and fewer reasons to go back to America. My beloved sister Alline died in 2010. As for my sons, well, they're adults with their own lives, and I'm only a phone call or a plane trip away. It made sense for me to embrace Switzerland, the country where I lived (and had lived for almost two decades), as my official home.

Let me tell you, it's much easier to be born the citizen of a country than to become one. I had to pass a difficult test, so difficult that I prepared by studying with a teacher. Among other things, I had to learn Swiss history and a little High German, the most correct (and difficult) form of the language. Then, I had to appear before a committee that would evaluate my candidacy. I asked if Erwin could accompany me on my big day, but I was told no, just the applicant.

I walked into the room and found myself face-to-face with seven judges. I've performed in front of millions of people and never felt apprehensive, not for one second, but in front of *this* group . . . well, I was terrified. Hoping to make a tense situation a little lighter, I immediately admitted to being very nervous. No reaction. Then I passed around candy I had purchased for the occasion, admittedly a desperate ploy, but who doesn't like candy? Especially in Switzerland. Still no reaction, and I thought, *Tina, the candy's not working either.* The committee was taking its job very seriously. I was on my own.

———

A man with a heavy voice said, "Tina, do you realize that you have to speak the language before you can apply for citizenship?"

"Yes," I answered, eager to please. "I can tell you who I am, where I came from, and how many children I have, in High German." Sort of. I could try, and if I needed help, I was allowed to consult a little booklet of answers. Maybe I was being paranoid, but I swear that one of the younger interviewers was staring at me, trying to make me feel more nervous than I already was.

I took a deep breath and said, "*Ich bin* Tina Turner."

To answer the next question, I had to peek in the book. I remembered to ask, "May I?"—"*Darf ich?*" My teacher constantly reminded me that the Swiss are sticklers for manners, *always* ask permission—and I did that successfully, too.

The final question was the most difficult. "Can you tell us something you know about Switzerland?"

My mind went blank, until I remembered that recently I had been at a party with someone who was describing "*Schweizerpsalm*," the Swiss national anthem. The person observed that it was very church-like—more like a hymn than a typically patriotic song, and "*Schweizerpsalm*" actually means "Swiss psalm." On the spot, I decided to make this the subject of my answer. "I'm in the process of learning the national anthem," I said with authority, "and I think it's interesting that it sounds so religious, like something that you'd hear in a church."

The interviewer was taken aback. He wouldn't have been at all surprised if I'd started talking about DJ BoBo, a Swiss rock singer, but he never expected Tina Turner to bring up the national anthem, the country's most hallowed piece of music. Turns out it was the perfect answer. Once again, I was saved by a song. The committee approved my application, and I became the proud holder of a Swiss passport.

For some reason, word of my new nationality spread quickly and was of great interest to people other than myself. There was such a clamor, along with endless speculation that I must have done it for tax reasons, which wasn't true. I think that living in a country for seventeen years—with the person you love—is reason enough to call it home, especially when the person you love is about to become your husband.

I hope the details of our wedding are as fresh in your mind as they are in mine, although I'm not sure if my description has done it justice. When I close my eyes, I can still smell the heavenly flowers. I'm probably not the first bride to watch her wedding DVD over and over again, which is what I do, and every time I press "play," I notice a detail I missed before.

The fairy tale continued the day after the wedding, when Erwin and I set out for our honeymoon at the Grand Hotel a Villa Feltrinelli on Lake Garda in Italy. We were driving there, and we left the garlands of "just married" flowers on the front of the car, a sweet, traditional touch for a mature couple. It started pouring (thank God it didn't the day before!), and the flowers got so wet and heavy we had to stop and take them off. The hotel was a perfect place for a honeymoon, with a romantic boathouse we had all to ourselves.

We traded one beautiful location for another when we met Oprah at the legendary Grand-Hôtel du Cap-Ferrat in the South of France, to shoot a series of interviews for *Oprah's Next Chapter.*

Only Oprah could persuade a bride to abandon her honeymoon. I agreed, partly because we have so much fun together, and partly because I wanted to talk about my old life one last time before I started my new life as Mrs. Erwin Bach. I was willing to discuss anything, including my time with Ike, hoping to put it to bed once and for all.

I had spent the past couple of years planning, organizing, and preparing, I told Oprah confidently, describing the reasons behind my retirement, my frenzy of downsizing, and my determination to focus on what was truly important. I claimed I was taking control of my life. Do you know the wonderful expression "If you want to make God laugh, tell him your plans"? Looking back, that's what comes to mind, because "control" is the last word I would use to describe what happened to me. Just three months after the wedding, on an ordinary October morning, when I should have been happily heading off for a vacation in Marrakesh with friends, I was slammed with a devastating reminder of my own mortality.

I woke up, opened my eyes, and tried to speak, but I couldn't get any words out. Erwin, who is always coolheaded in times of crisis, knew that there was something terribly wrong and immediately called my physician, Professor Doctor Vetter, who told him to give me an aspirin and rush me to the hospital. I kept thinking I was fine. In fact, when I was met with a wheelchair at the entrance to the hospital, I resisted getting into it, surrendering only after the doctor insisted that a wheelchair would get me upstairs faster. The orderlies put me on a table, tucked me under a blanket, and I thought, *I guess we're not going on that trip to Marrakesh.* Somehow, I didn't understand that my condition was very serious, that I'd suffered a stroke.

Deny, deny, deny.

I was so oblivious to what was happening that when I found myself alone in the room, I decided to get up. I swung my legs over the side of the table, and immediately fell down and hit the floor. That's when I discovered I couldn't stand on my own. *Oh my God, what have I done?* I said to myself, as if I had been responsible for my collapse. *And how can I fix this?* was my next question. Unfortunately, I didn't have any answers, and I was too embarrassed to call for help. Legs for days and muscles of steel from dancing, but I didn't have the strength to get up. Terrified, I dragged myself over to a sofa and somehow managed to pull my body into a sitting position, all the while thinking that I couldn't imagine Tina Turner paralyzed. Eventually, I fell asleep.

The next day, Professor Doctor Vetter told me that I'd had a stroke. This time, I heard him. The stroke had delivered a powerful blow to my body. My entire right side was numb. He explained that I would have to work with a physiotherapist to learn how to walk again, and that using my right hand would be a problem. I even had to be taught a special way to get up if I fell down. I was beginning to understand that I would fall down . . . a lot.

In the normal course of events, we're carefree, adventurous children when we first learn how to walk, and we have enormous self-confidence because we haven't encountered the obstacles life puts in our way. But if you have to learn how to walk when you're an adult, you know exactly what can happen if you fall, and it's never good. It's also humiliating. I felt so weak, so helpless. I doubted that I would ever be able to wear high heels again, let alone dance in them.

I stayed in the hospital for about ten days, and during that time I pulled myself together. I'm a fighter, I reminded myself. I always have been. I swore I would never give in—that I would *make* my leg walk again, that I would teach it and reteach it, until I could stand on my own two feet. I willed myself to do things because, in my life, I always had to push and push, and go and go. It worked, but nothing about the rehabilitation process was easy.

As much as I wanted to focus on my recovery, I had to think about what was happening in the outside world. There were rumors circulating. "Tina Turner Recovering from a Stroke." "Tina Turner Has a Mysterious Illness." If the news spread, I would be surrounded by paparazzi and a crowd of concerned fans would mount a vigil at my door. It wasn't about vanity, although I knew tabloid reporters would knock each other out for the chance to take a picture of me in my miserable condition. I just couldn't handle the distraction. It would be one more problem to solve, when I was trying desperately to solve so many. I denied everything. We told no one.

A few weeks after my stroke, while still recovering under the supervision of my doctors, I turned to TCM (traditional Chinese medicine) for help getting back on my feet. My face and the way I walked had been affected by the episode. Sylvie Ackerman, my TCM therapist, suggested acupuncture—especially in the facial area, several times a week. I learned that the goal in TCM is to balance the body's energies—yin and yang, plus and minus—like a battery. I'm very aware of my body, and I noticed every change and improvement I experienced after each session. I called it "taking little, wonderful steps back in life." When I saw how helpful TCM was, I made it a regular part of my life.

Nevertheless, the physical effects of my stroke would last a long time. To this day, I have difficulty writing a signature that is legible, so autographs are out of the question. But the psychological effects were even more profound. The first time I was aware that something wasn't quite right in my body was on my wedding day, when I experienced discomfort in my neck and chest after the ceremony. The pain wasn't dramatic, and it went away as mysteriously as it came, but I started to think that maybe it was a sign. A sign of what? Age? A serious health problem? And now I'd had a stroke, which seemed like something that should happen to an old, unhealthy person, not me.

I was miserable. The battle for recovery left me with no strength or vitality. And I wasn't just dealing with the aftermath of the stroke. My doctor was concerned that my high blood pressure might be affecting my kidneys, so he referred me to a kidney specialist. Dr. Jörg Bleisch, an expert nephrologist, advised that my kidneys were performing at only 35 percent of their normal function. Concerned, he said that we would have to monitor them carefully, and he prescribed more medication to control my high blood pressure.

While I was processing the disturbing news about my ailing kidneys, I began another chapter in what was turning out to be a long-running health soap opera. The new crisis started a year after my stroke, during a vacation in Greece. I'm a huge fan of movies like *Clash of the Titans*, and any stories that have to do with gods, monsters, and Greek mythology, so I was eager to see the classic Greek landscape come to life. There I was, exploring the ruins and enjoying antiquity, when suddenly I felt dizzy, breathless, sick to my stomach. The sensation literally knocked me off my feet.

I discovered that I had vertigo, what the Swiss call *"Schwindel,"* an extreme balance disorder, and it was unnerving and frightening. The fearless Tina, who'd climbed the Eiffel Tower and danced on a moving crane, occasionally faking a fall just to see the panicked look on her manager's face (sorry, Roger), couldn't hold up her head without feeling sick. I couldn't stand, walk, or focus. In fact, any kind of motion was my enemy. My body was spinning out of control, and my world was spinning with me.

This was a new kind of sick, and I had to get help right away. Luckily, I was living in the country with the world's best health care system. Vertigo, which is often dismissed as "dizziness" and is an unexplored condition in many places, is a major area of study in Zurich, practically in my own backyard. I was sent to Professor Doctor Dominik Straumann, a neurologist at a special research facility, the Interdisciplinary Center for Vertigo and Neurological Visual Disorders, for evaluation. The experts decided that the reason I was so uncomfortable was that a tiny crystal deep in my ear canal (the term is "otoconia") had gotten loose and needed to be anchored, a complicated and potentially painful process.

There's a more scientific explanation, but the doctors determined my treatment would be *the chair*. I was led through an underground tunnel to a private area in the basement of the university. The first time I saw the chair I made a joke, "Is this where Frankenstein's monster sits?" It resembled something out of a science experiment—a massive piece of equipment that looked like it belonged at NASA, or on a futuristic roller coaster. *Do they expect me to climb into this thing and take a ride?* I thought. My doctor, along with his two assistants, helped me up, strapped me in, and turned it on.

The "chair" in question is actually a 3-D turntable which operates as a three-axis stimulator, as I'm told. It spins around in all directions and at all angles. In my case, the goal was to force my stray crystal—the source of my vertigo—back into its proper position. Then, my doctors promised, the disorienting sickness would stop. There I sat, bound to the machine, hurling through space, hands clenched, feet in the air, upside-down, sideways, every which way, eyes wide open, so the doctors could study my irises for indications that the treatment was working. "Don't move, Tina," they said repeatedly—which sounded a little funny because usually people expect me to *keep* moving. But, believe me, humor was not my first response while strapped to that chair. I felt a nausea so deep and intense that it went through to my very soul. I had to go back to the chair for several sessions, and each time afterward I asked myself, "How did I ever survive that?" I felt destroyed. When it was really bad, Erwin had to leave me at the clinic to spend the night because I was too sick to make the short trip home.

It was a happy day when the elusive crystal responded to the chair's gravity-defying swings and settled into position, signaling the end of my vertigo. The procedure took so much out of me that I sat in a wheelchair for almost a month. It did threaten to come back once, but I summoned up every ounce of strength in my body and forced myself to fight back. As soon as I felt the familiar signs of an episode, I tried to keep still, knowing the whole time that the evil *Schwindel* was waiting, whispering, "If you move the wrong way, I'm coming." My whole body broke out in a sweat as I fought the sensation. It was almost like staring down a dog whose eyes say, "If you move, I'll bite you." But I held firm, resisting, willing it to go away.

I won the fight, and I was proud of myself, not realizing that there were bigger battles ahead. Battles that would leave me wondering, *How did I go from being the picture of health, a cover girl, a bride for God's sake, to Job?*

With every visit to Dr. Bleisch, who was trying to contain my high blood pressure, I developed a growing awareness that something was wrong with my kidneys. I tried to understand the kidneys' purpose, and why it was important. Something, if I'm being honest, I'd never thought about before. I suspect that most people don't know where their organs are located, or what they do, until they find themselves in the middle of a medical crisis.

Let's not forget, we had a language barrier. I speak very little German, so the doctors had to explain complex medical issues to me in English, which was a foreign language to them. It wasn't easy, but they were very patient with me and did an outstanding job.

The simple explanation is that the kidneys house the body's filtration system and are responsible for cleaning about 450 gallons of blood every day. In the course of a very complicated process, blood moves through filtering units, which are called "glomeruli," and waste products are removed and ultimately excreted in urine. When the system is working properly, we're not even aware that it's happening. But if the kidneys fail and can no longer prevent the buildup of waste, salt, or extra fluid, the body can be in serious trouble.

If that happens, there is the need for "renal replacement therapy," either a kidney transplant or dialysis. The gold standard in this situation is a kidney transplant. One fully functioning kidney can take the place of two. With a new kidney, a person can have a very good chance of leading a near-normal life. Kidney transplant recipients live longer than those on dialysis, and they feel better, too.

The other option is dialysis, either hemodialysis or peritoneal dialysis. Mostly hemodialysis is used, which usually takes place in a hospital, or a dialysis center. It involves going three times a week, for about four hours at a time, while a machine filters toxins and excess fluid from the blood.

Mind you, I'm not sure how much of this information my mind was absorbing at the time. When you're sick, it's so easy to not hear what doctors are telling you—out of fear, resistance, and yes, denial. Even when I was vaguely aware of terms like "transplant," or "dialysis," I didn't think I was in immediate danger.

The plan was to focus on improving, or at least stabilizing, my kidneys. There's that word again, *plan*. Not so fast, Tina. You know what happens when you start talking about a plan. It usually means a curveball is on the way, and it was. I was blindsided by news of yet another medical complication, and this was a big one. For months, I had been suffering from the condition no one wants to talk about: chronic diarrhea. I was so weak, and my system was so unpredictable, that I couldn't leave the house anymore. Actually, I could barely leave the second floor. It took all of my strength to stagger the short distance between the bedroom and the bathroom. I felt like a prisoner and I looked terrible. I barely recognized myself. I was lucky to have Erwin at my side when I needed him the most.

In January 2016, I was shocked to be diagnosed with intestinal cancer—a carcinoma and several malignant polyps, early stage. At this point, we didn't know if the cancer *could* be removed, let alone if there would be any next steps. The days of uncertainty were dreadful. I crept around the house, restlessly moving from one room to another. I stared at the lake, the walls, my photographs from the past, even the piano, although there was no music in my life. "Aren't you sorry you married an old woman," I cried to Erwin, because we seemed to spend all of our time going from one doctor to another. Fortunately, he had a really good attitude. Erwin always radiated confidence, optimism, and joie de vivre, and he was like that from the first time I met him. With his help, I tried to keep calm during this upsetting roller-coaster ride.

The good thing about a roller-coaster ride is that it goes up as often as it goes down. I had surgery a month after my diagnosis, and the afflicted part of my intestine was removed. Luckily, the cancer had been detected early and it proved to be slow-moving. My doctors were optimistic that it could be cured, and I felt a glimmer of hope again. But just a glimmer, and only for a moment.

Dr. Bleisch explained that my kidneys were deteriorating and we now faced a medical dilemma. Cancer is terrible news under any circumstances, but in my case, the consequences turned out to be far-reaching. As a cancer patient, I would have to take medication to boost my immune system. The problem was that transplant patients are required to take "immunosuppressants," drugs that have the opposite effect of *suppressing* the body's immune system, so it won't reject the new organ. In other words, the two treatments are contradictory. The drugs used to control my cancer would be in direct conflict with the drugs necessary for a successful transplant, if my kidneys failed to the point where I needed one.

I was shocked to find myself in this awful, between-a-rock-and-a-hard-place position. In the back of my mind, I had hoped that if I ever experienced a true kidney catastrophe, a transplant might be a possibility. But Dr. Bleisch was telling me that, post cancer surgery, that option was unlikely. We would have to postpone any consideration of a transplant for at least a year. A year! As if I had a year. Of course, the bigger question was, where would I get a kidney if I needed one?

In this case, it did me no good to live in Switzerland. At the time, the country's organ donor rate (from deceased donors) was one of the lowest in Europe, meaning that if I signed up on the waiting list, my name would be there for an indeterminate period. I was seventy-five years old. Realistically, how much time did I have to wait until it was my turn? Would I even get a turn? Being a woman in my seventies made me an unlikely candidate. Being a woman in my seventies with *cancer* made my situation impossible. Once again, I found myself in a position with strong winds against me. Going to the black market for a kidney was out of the question. I never even considered it. But can you imagine any celebrity trying to buy an organ surreptitiously? It would probably end up on Instagram.

By July, my kidneys were so weak that Dr. Bleisch scheduled me to start dialysis a short time later. I was completely opposed to the idea. "Oh no, no, no," I told him. "I'm not living on a machine." It wasn't my idea of life.

But the toxins in my body had started taking over. I couldn't eat. I had little pimples all over my stomach. I was surviving, but not living. I guess that's what happens when you die, you just diminish slowly and slowly and slowly and slowly. In Buddhism, death is acceptance. *I'm not a young kid anymore*, I thought. Years ago, I might have said, "Oh, I don't want to die because I don't know what's ahead." At my age, I felt that I'd finished what I came here to do. Once you live this long, there's not much more ahead. If my kidneys were going, and it was time for me to die, I could accept that. I was just a little bit tired. I would go join my mother and my sister. And it was okay. When it's time, it's really time. We do live and die. I was ready to accept that.

I didn't mind the thought of dying—I've always been curious about the afterlife—but I was concerned about *how* I would go. One of the benefits of living in Switzerland is that assisted suicide is a legal act. After determining that a person is sane, a doctor can prescribe a lethal drug to a patient with "unbearable suffering." But the patient has to inject the drug him- or herself. As I understand it, a line is opened, you give yourself a nice little injection, or a drink, then you smile and go off to the other dimension to find out a few things. This sounded like a painless way to deal with a painful problem. There are several organizations that offer the service of coordinating the process, including Exit and Dignitas.

I signed up to be a member of Exit, just in case.

I think that's when the idea of my death became a reality for Erwin. He was very emotional about not wanting to lose me, not wanting me to leave. He said he didn't want another woman, or another life. We were happy and he would do anything to keep us together.

At this point, Erwin shocked me by saying that he wanted to give me one of his kidneys.

I could hardly believe it then, and there are times when I still can't believe it. I was overwhelmed by the enormity of his offer. Because I loved him, my first response was to try to talk him out of taking such a serious and irreversible step. He was a young man. Why should he take such a risk to give me, an older woman, a few extra years? He knew he could survive with one kidney. But what if something happened to him? What if he had a problem with *his* kidney someday? "Darling, you're young. Don't, don't, don't interfere with your life. Think about your own future," I urged.

But Erwin had made up his mind. When he thought about his future, he thought of me. "My future is our future," he told me. And he wasn't the least bit worried about the possibility of needing a kidney someday. He believed in the gift of giving. "If you give, you receive," he said, confident that the universe would take care of him.

I cried as we sat in our living room holding hands, looking out at the lake. Despite the fact that my doctors were discouraging about the possibility of a kidney transplant, I chose to believe that it could happen—that it *would* happen. At that moment, I felt something that had been missing from my life ever since this series of medical calamities—my stroke, my *Schwindel*, my cancer, and now this—started.

I felt hope.

11

"ASK ME HOW I FEEL"

" The night is awful cold, ask me how I feel "

S taying healthy—and honestly, staying alive—meant undergoing dialysis. I knew it was the right thing to do, the *only* thing to do, yet I was still unhappy about the notion of spending so much time hooked up to a machine. When I made an exploratory visit to the clinic, I warned my doctor, "I'm just taking a look at the equipment." In the dialysis room, I saw this R2D2 thing—a figure straight out of *Star Wars*—standing there, looking back at me. This little machine would take over my kidney functions. *Do I really want to do this?* I wondered. I had no choice. I didn't look forward to it, it was just something I had to do. This was my roundabout journey to a dialysis chair at a hospital in Zollikon, Switzerland.

My first day at the clinic, the doctor showed me where he was going to insert a catheter in my chest, so I could be connected to the dialysis machine. My first reaction was, "Well, I can't wear low cuts anymore because there's going to be a hole there!" I may have been sick, but I was still Tina, still thinking about fashion and looking good. I was told to watch out for infection at the catheter site, since it would stay in place as long as I was getting dialysis. Some of the other rules were to drink less liquid and to avoid contact with anyone who was sick.

The dialysis room was bright and unadorned (no, I didn't have any desire to redecorate it), and the furniture was covered with gray plastic to make it easier to keep it clean. The most distinctive detail about the room was the whooshing sound the pumps made when they were hooked up to patients. I experienced a whooshing feeling inside, too, as the fluids traveled through my body during dialysis. The sensation was so strong that it persisted for hours after the treatment, the way the body sometimes feels the rhythmic pull of waves after swimming in the ocean.

Some days were better than others. If they took out too much water during the cleansing process, I felt weak and tired when it was over, and I'd tell the nurses the next time I came in.

While I can't say I liked going to the clinic, or that I looked forward to it, I got used to being there. I think the nurses liked me because they expected Tina Turner to behave like a star—to be stand-offish and spoiled, and to make demands, which I never did. "You're so *nice*," they'd say with surprise. The other patients had a tendency to complain, which is to be expected, given that they were sick and uncomfortable. But I tried to carry a little fun with me. My feeling was that I had nothing to complain about—my husband was giving me a kidney, and I was so grateful for that! I kept reminding myself that I was lucky, not doomed, even though my list of illnesses seemed to get longer and longer.

For the next nine months, the dialysis chair was the center of my life. Having a routine helped. Knowing what to expect each time I went to the clinic made the process less upsetting. I learned to wear soft, comfortable clothes, and I often fell into a deep sleep for the first two hours because I was still weak and feeling poorly. When I woke up, Erwin and Didier, our majordomo, the lovely man who runs our household with dedication, skill, and grace, were at my side if I wanted company. I entertained myself with my books, which were always within reach, and I daydreamed the rest of the time.

I loved looking through my volume of photographs by a man named Horst P. Horst. The first time I saw his work I was in London (I think I was shopping at Molton Brown), and I looked up and was almost knocked off my feet by the gallery of framed images on the walls. I had never seen such beautiful photographs. They were the essence of elegance and glamour. I didn't care how much they cost, I had to have them. I hung them all over the house, and admired them every day. I brought a book of Horst's to the clinic because his greatest photographs, including a woman holding a fan, a corseted torso seen from the back, and a nude draped on a satin curtain, showed me that there was still beauty in the world—and they reminded me of home, where my Horsts were on display.

I've collected quite a library of books by Deepak Chopra because I'm a student of his ideas about consciousness, and the strong connection between mind and body. Meeting him in California confirmed my feeling that he is a very special soul on the planet, and his words always inspire me. I found *The Book of Secrets* especially comforting at the clinic because Chopra discusses how facing death can help a person to develop a real passion for being alive, a message that holds meaning for me today. Every now and then, when I have a moment, I go to my chanting room and sit there to read what he has to say, just collecting information and letting it soak in. I don't know what's coming in the next world, but I want to be prepared, and Deepak Chopra teaches us that the body and the mind have to develop extra, extra, extra to connect to the universe we can't see.

My interest in Dante is a little harder to explain, probably because Dante is harder to understand. You don't dare move when you read Dante! When I started going through his books—and that was before dialysis—I felt like I was standing on an egg with one foot, and that eggshell was going to break. I knew I'd have to read his writing over and over to comprehend what he was saying about the afterlife. *The Divine Comedy* suggests that on our journey to Heaven, we have to go through trials and tribulations to get to the top. If we learn, we progress to the next level. Every life has its tests, some more dramatic than others. I've had my share of tests, and I think I've learned from them, but who's to say I would *ever* reach the kind of enlightenment Dante describes. As difficult as it sounds, I'm determined to challenge myself and try.

When I didn't feel like reading, I let my mind wander wherever it wanted to go. How many times have I said, "I'm done with Ike"? Yet here I was, drifting through memories I'd kept buried for so long, my recollection of our wedding in Tijuana and that trip to see a sex show after, for example. In my chair, I had the time and motivation to look back, to watch the story of my life on "rewind," so to speak: time to contemplate the big questions. It sounds a little clichéd to say that you see your life pass before you when you think you're dying, but that's pretty much what happened to me.

The landscape shifted, as past and present merged. My mother and Ike were in my thoughts constantly while I was at the clinic. Nothing could change the truth—that I was abandoned by Muh and abused by Ike. Or that I spent too many years believing I would never be loved. But now I was developing a different perspective. I realized that as painful as these experiences were, they no longer defined me. After Erwin came into my life, my sad story became a love story. If anyone ever doubted that the feeling we had for each other was real, the great gift Erwin offered me—the gift of life—proved them wrong.

I was still taking drugs to control my high blood pressure, and

I began to resent them because I was certain they were making me feel worse. I remembered how life was before the pills, and I wished I could get back to feeling clearheaded and energetic, like *me*. When a friend suggested that I consider trying a different approach, and recommended a homeopathic doctor in France, I jumped at the chance.

I put my faith in another kind of healing. The homeopath suggested that my body was being affected adversely by toxins in the water supply at the Château Algonquin. I was so eager to try a new approach, no matter how far-fetched, that I replaced all the pipes in the house and had little devices installed so the water could be purified by crystals. My new doctor replaced my conventional medicines with homeopathic alternatives. Instead of taking pills, I was constantly drinking, drinking, drinking the treated water to combat my high blood pressure—and the new treatments actually made me feel better. Maybe it was bullshit, but I believed in it, and as I told Erwin, my attitude at the time was that it couldn't hurt. I knew these measures were a bit extreme, and that my established Swiss doctors would never approve of what I was doing, so I took the coward's way out. I simply didn't tell them that I had stopped taking my blood pressure medicine, or that I was experimenting with alternative treatments.

The trouble started when I went to see Dr. Bleisch for a checkup. About three months had gone by, and I was curious to see if the homeopathic treatments were lowering my blood pressure and improving the condition of my kidneys. I felt fine, so I expected good news. I casually admitted to Dr. Bleisch that I hadn't been taking my blood pressure medication—just gave it up—thinking the revelation was no big deal. Big mistake. Big, big, mistake. He seemed shocked, and he probably wanted to say, "You have really messed up." Instead, he asked incredulously, "Didn't you talk to your other doctors about this?" He explained that there can be serious complications for the kidney when a patient stops taking critical drugs.

Believe it or not, I didn't understand that unmanaged high blood pressure could accelerate my kidney damage until after my doctor told me what I learned that day, that my failure to treat my high blood pressure had essentially destroyed my kidneys. Of course, I would have lived differently if I had known; of course, I wouldn't have traded my medication for homeopathic alternatives if I'd realized there was so much at stake. The consequences of my ignorance ended up being a matter of life and death.

Suddenly, it became clear to me that a battle against illness is a battle for total and correct information. Maybe I was locking the proverbial barn door after the horse was stolen, but now it was important to me to try to understand what had happened to my body, so I could make better choices in the future. For example, I didn't know that kidney disease is considered a "silent killer"—by the time most people experience any symptoms of kidney failure, 80 percent of their kidney tissue has already been destroyed. My condition, high blood pressure, is one of the leading causes of kidney failure. Thinking back, I may not have had symptoms in the beginning, but some of the problems I later blamed on the medication—from feeling tired and sick, to being itchy—are definitely symptoms of end-stage kidney disease.

Oh, the questions I asked myself again and again. Why didn't I listen to my doctors? Whatever made me think that I was in a position to determine my own treatment? I wouldn't have traded my medication for homeopathic alternatives if I'd realized there was so much at stake. I'm not trying to say something bad against homeopathy. In fact, I was treated successfully by a homeopathic doctor after I was diagnosed with tuberculosis in 1969. I believed in balancing my body and having the toxins cleansed from my blood, and I did it for years. It worked for me when I was young, but when I got older, and had a serious, long-term illness that was dependent on conventional medicine, it was unlikely that homeopathy could help me. If only I hadn't discontinued the medication. If, if, if! Such a small decision, but one that would continue to haunt me.

With my usual optimism, I wanted to know how I could *fix* this, if there was anything I could do to revive my kidneys. But I was told that there was no way to reverse the negative effects of what I'd done to myself. By December 2016, my kidneys were at a new low of 20 percent. "Does this mean death?" I asked, letting the obvious answer sink in.

At this terrible moment of guilt, self-recrimination, and yes, regret, I learned something wonderful about Erwin. He never reproached me for my mistake, not with a word or a glance. Instead, he was loyal, kind, and understanding. More importantly, he was determined to help me get through all this alive.

Because my numbers were plunging so rapidly and we were in a race against time, the solution that had seemed like such a long shot only recently—a kidney transplant—became my only possible salvation. I underwent a second colonoscopy to determine if any cancer cells remained in my intestines and, miraculously, received a diagnosis of "all clear." Since I no longer had to worry about contradictory treatments—immunoboosters vs. immunosuppressants—and we had Erwin's kidney, we could start the process of preparing for the transplant.

Erwin and I thought very carefully about which Swiss hospital to choose for the surgery: there were several strong possibilities. We selected the University Hospital of Basel because it was recommended by friends and trusted experts. Also, I had a gut feeling about the place when we visited for the first time. I felt safe there. We liked the staff, everyone seemed very professional, and we had full confidence in Professor Doctor Jürg Steiger, the doctor in charge of my case; Professor Doctor Gürke, my surgeon; and Thomas Vögele, the hospital coordinator who would attend to all the details.

While they were studying me, I was studying *them*, and I was impressed by what I saw. There were pleasant human touches in Professor Doctor Steiger's office, including photographs of his children and a picture of a farm, which turned out to have special significance for him because it depicted the mountainous region that was home to his mother and her family. He struck me as being a happy man, always cheerful and positive even when we were discussing very serious matters. I found his attitude reassuring. When he looked at me, he made me feel as if he saw the whole *person*, not only the illness.

Preparing for a kidney transplant is a huge undertaking for both the recipient and the donor, and the hardest part comes long before the surgeon makes an incision. Erwin's magnanimous decision to give me one of his kidneys was the first step in a long and involved approval process. Since the year 2000, nearly half of all kidney transplants performed in Switzerland have been "living donor" transplants, when a person voluntarily gives one of their organs to someone who needs it. There are strict guidelines. In the early days of transplantation, a living donor had to be a blood relative, a parent, a sibling, a child. It wasn't until 1991 that married (or unmarried) partners and friends could donate their organs.

Yes, it was critical that Erwin's kidney be a good match for me, and extensive medical tests would determine our compatibility. But the standard approval process also included a thorough "psycho-social evaluation," or series of psychological tests, to establish Erwin's state of mind. Why was he willing to be a donor? What was our relationship? How did he make the decision? How did he deal with stress? These were just a few of the questions he had to answer.

The interview process is rigorous because doctors sometimes come across a donor who has given up an organ for the wrong reasons. They mentioned a farmer's wife who donated a kidney to her husband, only to file for divorce as soon as she left the hospital. Her attitude was, "I've done my duty, now I can leave you for good." In her mind, she was using her kidney to buy her freedom.

In the back of my mind, I wondered if anyone would think that Erwin's living donation was transactional in some way. Incredibly, considering how long we had been together, there were still people who wanted to believe that Erwin married me for my money and fame. What else would a younger man want with an older woman? Erwin and I knew it wasn't true, and he always ignored the rumors and wasn't bothered by them. In my weakened state, they made me crazy. Erwin never cared about any of that—he cared about me. As I'd expected, after talking to Erwin, the doctors determined he was not giving me his kidney for financial gain, and he was fully aware of any risk. Erwin knew exactly what he was doing. Erwin *always* knows exactly what he's doing: that's his nature. His offer to give me his kidney was the ultimate gift, a gift of love.

After Erwin's physical exam, the doctors confirmed what I had known for years—he was in fabulous shape. In fact, he was so healthy that they rated his biological age as lower than his actual age (which, in my mind, still didn't make him younger than me because he still had the same habit of turning off the lights and closing the doors at night, just like an old man!). I joked that with Erwin's kidney in my body, I'd be able to run a marathon.

The medical tests the doctors gave us were extensive. Erwin and I have the same blood type—type A—so that was a good start. But there were other considerations. I'm making the process sound way too simple, but we were tested for tissue typing, which indicates how many antigens the donor shares with the recipient, and cross-matching, which predicts how the recipient will react to the new kidney. A positive cross match is actually bad news because it means the recipient's body would attack the new organ, and a transplant would not be possible. We passed the tests, so we had a strong foundation for a successful transplant.

Meanwhile, Erwin and I had to stay healthy. All I could hear was the clock ticking. I couldn't afford to lose a bit of my strength, energy, or courage. Of course, I worried that there would be another delay or, God forbid, another problem, and I wasn't getting any younger. We were relieved to receive the news that we could move forward. I was so ready, I literally started counting the days.

We traveled back and forth to Basel, which is about two hours from Zurich by car, to meet with the transplant team. Basel is one of the largest cities in Switzerland, and it's located on the Rhine, one of the major rivers in Europe. I'm fascinated by the sight of water, which is ironic because I can't swim. My appreciation is purely aesthetic. When I'm home, I love looking at Lake Zurich: experiencing the different colors; seeing that it sometimes goes this way or that way, or is perfectly still; watching the reflection of the sky.

I felt the same way about watching the currents of the Rhine during our visits to Basel. There are days when the river is lazy and flows slowly through the city, and other days when the water rages, wild and dangerous. But mostly I loved watching the Rhine because it reminded me of our happy days in Cologne, where the river is an important part of life. The time Erwin and I shared there was a new beginning for us, not only as a couple, but for me personally, because I was free and truly in love for the first time. Being on its banks always gave me a sense of well-being. I saw young people everywhere, bathing and having fun. Life in all its glory! I hoped the Rhine once again represented a new beginning for me, as it had in the past.

In Basel, Erwin planned our arrival so we could slip in and out of the hospital without being recognized, just as he did at the dialysis clinic in Zurich. He parked in the underground garage and took me by the hand to the tunnel that led to the main building. The tunnel was long—about two hundred meters—and it formed a sort of boundary between the world outside the hospital and the world in it. To me, it was symbolic, just like the River Styx, the river between the worlds of life and death in Dante's *Inferno*. I felt uneasy the whole time we were in it, and I eagerly watched for landmarks that indicated we were nearing the exit. First, we passed the Coca-Cola machine, then the red walls that gradually turned gray, and finally we arrived at the elevator that carried us up into the main lobby of the hospital—there was no back entrance. We moved swiftly and silently, and I usually wore a hood. Somehow, we managed to walk past hundreds of people without ever being stopped for a selfie. Only in Switzerland!

Once more, Professor Doctor Steiger carefully explained everything we needed to know about the transplantation process. And once again, I found that I was the "cat with nine (maybe ten) lives." I was already a high-risk patient because of my recent cancer, but the risk escalated when tests showed that my heart had been damaged by so many years of high blood pressure: the muscle was enlarged and the vessels calcified. There was some question as to whether or not a weak heart could withstand the stress of surgery. The news was troubling, but I was getting used to setbacks, and I refused to let this one dim my enthusiasm.

Professor Doctor Steiger saw that I was strong *and* strong-willed. Ultimately, he decided that my heart was up to the job, so he green-lighted the transplant, scheduling our big day for April 7, 2017. Our doctors were amazed by how relaxed and open-minded Erwin was as we got closer to the surgery. Most donors get really nervous, sometimes to the point where they're more frightened than the person receiving the organ. Not Erwin. He was upbeat and unflappable every step of the way. I can't say the same about me. My body had been through so much physical and emotional stress that my moods were unpredictable. I sometimes felt depressed, which made me feel guilty, because I knew I should be counting my blessings.

A tremendous amount of planning was necessary to set up the two procedures. Two operating theaters are required—one for the donor and one for the recipient—two surgical teams, two of everything. Erwin's operation would take place first. For the past few years, our fears and hopes had centered around *my* condition—my stroke, my high blood pressure, my cancer. While I was understandably anxious about the transplant, I was far more concerned about my Erwin, who was about to have a kidney cut out of his body . . . for me. I could barely listen to the description of the "retroperitoneoscopic nephrectomy," as his procedure was called. The kidney, which is covered in a layer of protective, fatty tissue, is exposed, the renal artery, the renal vein, and the ureter are clipped, and the kidney is removed, flushed with a cold special liquid, placed on ice in a dish, and rushed to the recipient for transplantation.

I didn't want to think about any of these gory details when Erwin was wheeled into his operating room. After about an hour, the surgeon signaled that preparation of the recipient could begin, and suddenly it was my turn. I was given some medication to calm me, then the nurses lifted me from my bed up onto the operating table. The room was bright and busy with activity. People kept asking me my name and why I was there, to make sure they had the right patient for the right surgery. Then, a young man attached electrodes to my chest and hooked up an access device to my vein. The ventilator pumped, the anesthesia started to flow, my eyelids fluttered and closed, and I was out.

The next thing I knew, the nurses were calling my name, trying to wake me up. I seemed to be lying in the same position as when I'd closed my eyes, but hours had passed. I was told that the surgery was over and the doctors were happy. I was so groggy that everything— lights, sounds, smatterings of conversation, visits from doctors and nurses—felt dreamlike. It took me a while to understand that I was in Intensive Care, surrounded by what seemed like a hundred machines, starting my new life as a woman with a healthy kidney.

I was more coherent when I woke up the next day. I was so excited that the operation was over, and after a few tentative stretches of my fingers and toes, I realized that I felt fine. The best moment was when Erwin, the most beautiful sight, came rolling into my room in his wheelchair. He somehow managed to look good, even handsome, as he greeted me with an energetic "Hi, darling!" I was so emotional—happy, overwhelmed, and relieved that we had come through it alive.

With the surgery safely behind us, I was ready to hear all about it. The doctors told me that Erwin was stretched out on his side the whole time, while I was on my back. From start to finish, it took about two and a half hours, although the critical part of the procedure, the actual transplant, was accomplished in a matter of minutes. I found it interesting that my useless kidneys had been left in place, which is standard practice. Now I had three kidneys! I got chills as they described the dramatic moment when my blood started flowing through Erwin's kidney and my new organ lit up bright red with signs of life. It was like magic.

Erwin and I enjoyed a flawless recovery. His room was right next to mine, and we brought a lot of light and laughter to that hospital, especially when Erwin wheeled himself over to my room and held court. The staff was used to caring for people who were old and sick. But Erwin, this vibrant, younger man giving his older wife a kidney, was so full of life and charm that he was a welcome diversion. It amused Professor Doctor Steiger that my husband surrounded himself with stacks of car magazines, which he read obsessively. Clearly, Erwin was already planning his next road trip.

Professor Doctor Gürke, my surgeon, was pretty impressed with my recovery. I was able to be discharged after only seven days because I was strong and my doctors didn't foresee any problems. Erwin's recovery was even faster. He snapped right back to his old self, and within a few weeks was enjoying his first glass of wine. He's been full speed ahead ever since then.

When I say full speed, I mean *full speed*. Six months after his surgery, he jumped on his Harley-Davidson and set off on a road tour of America with his biker friends. Subsequently, we went back to the hospital in Basel for a checkup, and Erwin complained that his neck was bothering him. "Yes, Mr. Bach," the doctor said. "But that's not related to surgery, or age, or anything like that, that's related to your Harley!"

I, on the other hand, have experienced ups and downs. My body keeps trying to reject the new kidney, which is not uncommon after a transplant. It means I have to take strong doses of immunosuppressants to weaken my antibodies and prevent them from attacking an organ they don't recognize. Sometimes, the treatment involves spending more time in the hospital, and it comes with some unpleasant side effects, including dizziness, forgetfulness, anxiety, and the occasional bout of insane diarrhea. Ironically, when I feel dizzy it is because of *low* blood pressure, which is an entirely new sensation. I have to take a lot of pills—at one point, I was taking as many as twenty a day—and I do it very carefully, knowing that I can't make any mistakes.

In 2017, as the holidays approached, I started feeling more energetic. I was looking forward to my birthday on November 26, which we planned to celebrate with our closest friends at our country house. I always enjoy getting birthday cards, notes, and now emails commemorating the occasion, but this year was particularly meaningful to me because Erwin and I had come through so much. I'm not trying to tempt fate—I know that my medical adventure is far from over. After a transplant, it seems that there's always another doctor's appointment, test, or biopsy on the schedule. But I'm still here—*we're* still here, closer than we ever imagined—and that's cause for celebration.

Erwin knew that the old Tina (or maybe I was the new-and-improved Tina) was back when I got excited about ordering new end tables for the living room. Then, I pulled out the ornaments and transformed our home into a Christmas wonderland. For me, the urge to decorate is a sure sign of life.

After so many years of being sick, frightened, desperate, resigned, I felt the joy of the holiday, the joy of living.

12

"PARADISE IS HERE"

" The future is this moment, not some place out there "

While I was battling my various illnesses, Erwin surprised me by announcing that we were expecting visitors. He had invited nine, maybe ten, people to come to the Château Algonquin that very night to talk to me about developing *Tina: The Tina Turner Musical*, a stage show based on the story of my life. I wanted to say, "No! No! No! I did it, I did it, I did it—I've done it." I had no interest in revisiting the past, let alone hearing people sing about it. But it was too late. The meeting was set and the people had traveled a long way to see me, so I had to be polite and listen to them.

I was from the world of rock 'n' roll, so musical theater was a bit of a mystery to me. Trying to make conversation, I asked Joop van den Ende, one of the producers, "What's the difference between a musical and a great rock concert?" When he told me that a musical is a story told through songs, I saw the similarities between the two. I knew *Tina: The Tina Turner Musical* was destined to happen, because my life is *quite* a story, a story with songs. Ultimately, the idea started to make sense to me. I believed that the people involved in the musical, including award-winning director Phyllida Lloyd, who staged the musical *Mamma Mia!*, and writer Katori Hall (who, like me, is from Tennessee), would do a good job.

I gave *Tina: The Tina Turner Musical* my blessing and put one foot in first, then the other. I sat with producer Tali Pelman and became actively involved in the process to get the story right; not necessarily the facts—how and when something actually happened—but the feelings. When a biography is adapted for the stage, especially as a musical where characters sometimes sing instead of speaking, things are compressed and shuffled around; that's dramatic license. But I didn't care as long as the emotions were true. It was extremely important to me that the musical capture my authentic spirit, through good times and bad, and celebrate my lifelong relationship with my music and my audience. I didn't want the show to be about a woman who becomes a star. That's a small subject. My biography is *life*, the life of a woman who started as a little girl from Nutbush, who, as I've said many times, had strong winds against her, yet she stepped out into the big world with nothing but her voice, her optimism, and her will to survive.

Of course, the big question was, who would play Tina? After a search, a wonderful young actress named Adrienne Warren was cast in the role. She had to learn her songs, master her gestures and steps, find the right facial expressions, and develop the character—all in the shadow of the *real* Tina. I didn't want to make Adrienne nervous, but I did want to guide her.

Becoming Tina involves more than putting on a wig, a short skirt, and high heels, although the right costumes help. "First of all," I told her, "you have to realize that everyone will be a bit picky about you being Tina. You can't worry about what people think in terms of that. You're not Tina. My fans sat there at every tour, every show, and they know every move I ever made as well as I do. So don't just mimic me. Learn, but you have to be a little bit yourself, and then step into the shoes and become it totally." Adrienne had to find her "inner Tina."

I could tell her what I was feeling at different moments in my life, give her tips about phrasing and hitting the right notes, show her how to shake her hips from side to side instead of front to back, and demonstrate the intricacies of the Pony. But the most important lesson I could teach her was to *always* think about her audience—to concentrate on what they're feeling. "When you look out, and see that the audience is really into you, that they're having a good time, you have to hold on to that feeling and let it motivate you to be as good as Tina ever was." I told her she had to take their enthusiasm and give it right back to them, like a gift. My longest love affair has been with my audience.

If I thought for one second that, after my transplant, *finally* I'd earned the right to lounge in one of my beautifully upholstered antique chairs and eat Swiss chocolates, I discovered that Erwin had other ideas about how I should spend my time. After so much planning, the moment had come to officially announce *Tina: The Tina Turner Musical* and to get the show ready for its opening, and he expected me to be with it every step of the way. As if that wasn't enough, Erwin was also encouraging me to write this memoir *and* to be the subject of a documentary.

I've been blessed with a wonderful career, and when I decided to retire, it was because I was truly ready to leave public life. I didn't need a musical (or a book, or a documentary). However, what made me think twice was that I get so many cards and letters from people who tell me how much my story means to them. I feel that my story is my legacy, and I have to pass it on. It also occurred to me that there were things left unsaid in the past, and I should finally say them in my own voice.

I wanted to relax and truly enjoy my recovery and my retirement. But, as much as I kicked and screamed (well, maybe I never screamed), I understood what my husband was up to and I loved him for it. As he'd expected, when I was sick and fighting despair, thinking about the musical helped me stay focused and gave me something to look forward to. And after my surgery, working on the book gave me a chance to relive my memories—both good and bad—and to articulate some of the insights that came to me while I was thinking about my life. Basically, Erwin kept me busy so that I would keep going, and his plan worked.

My goal was to be in great shape by October 18, 2017, when we would announce the show and present Adrienne Warren to the media for the first time, and to be in even *better* shape for the official opening on April 17, 2018. This was an ambitious undertaking considering that I'd had major transplant surgery only six months earlier.

Honestly, I was worried that I wouldn't be able to do it. My face was swollen from taking cortisone. The drugs made me feel foggy. Sometimes it was hard to remember things. My energy level was up and down. My emotions were unpredictable. Then, when my body threatened to reject Erwin's kidney, and I found myself going back and forth to Basel for more rounds of tests and hospital visits to prevent that, I doubted that I would be ready to appear in front of cameras and a crowd of journalists at the October launch.

What if I had to be in a wheelchair? How could I face my fans? Would they accept me this way? I was worried.

Even though my recovery was slow, somehow, I pulled myself together. Dressed in a trim black Armani jacket, a bright red shirt, and black pants, I stood beside Adrienne and, together, we performed the opening of "Proud Mary." While she remained onstage to finish the song, I moved to the side to sit and watch. I was so pleased by her performance that I danced (and sang) along with her. I had good feelings about the musical *and* my first public appearance.

The official opening of *Tina: The Tina Turner Musical* six months later was at the Aldwych, one of London's oldest theaters. I wasn't seeing the show for the first time that night, but there would be critics in the audience, and it was impossible not to be a little nervous because I knew they would be watching me, trying to gauge my reaction. I dressed carefully, choosing a black Armani tuxedo. I wear classic clothes in my real life, and I wanted my outfit to be understated. For a touch of drama, I added an elegant pair of black Armani demi-gloves.

The evening was off to a funny start when we left the hotel. Fans on bicycles followed our car all the way to the theater, hoping to persuade me to sign autographs. I managed to do one or two, a struggle since my stroke, then passed through the crowds surrounding the Aldwych.

I was so surprised when people stood and applauded as I walked into the theater. I felt a little shy because all I could think of was *Why are you applauding me? I'm not the one who's going to be onstage!* Ultimately, I understood that the audience was telling me "It's your life and tonight we are celebrating it." There was not one empty seat, and I was happy to see some familiar faces in the house, from Rod Stewart (looking every bit the gentleman rock star) and Mark Knopfler, to our dear friends from Switzerland.

I sat down, trying to prepare myself mentally and emotionally for the show. Lights down, curtain up, and then came the sound I know as well as my own breath—*Nam-myoho-renge-kyo*—the Buddhist chant that is as much a part of me as my name. The first number, "Nutbush

City Limits" (which, you remember, is the song I wrote), got the show off to a rousing, foot-stomping start.

How strange to see the people in my life as characters—Mama Georgie, my grandmother—*love that you're with me tonight!* My mother, my sister, my children, Rhonda, Roger, and, of course, Ike. And Erwin, my husband, the character onstage and the real man sitting beside me, ready to squeeze my hand at my first sign of discomfort.

No matter how many times I'd imagined the various scenes in my mind, there was no way to anticipate the experience of watching my life performed onstage. I felt the substance of every word, yet entire scenes and whole songs passed by in an instant. Some moments stood out, one especially, because, in retrospect, it turned out to be a major turning point in my life—the first time I imagined a world without Ike.

Listening to "River Deep—Mountain High," I realized that it is more than just a song for me: it's an anthem. When I started working with Phil Spector, and heard him say, "Just the melody, Tina," I saw that there could be another way of singing—another way of living. I didn't know it at the time because I couldn't see into the future, but I came out of that collaboration transformed, with a taste of independence, an unaccustomed sense of self-worth, and an audience in Europe, where they embraced the song that America didn't know how to appreciate. After that song, a line was drawn. Never again would I settle for Ike's way, because I knew better, and I wanted more.

"River Deep—Mountain High" was a high point in my life, and it's a high point in the show, imaginatively staged by Phyllida and powerfully performed by Adrienne. I was transported and I think the rest of the audience was, too.

I think people were most curious about how I would react to the scenes of domestic violence that are an integral part of my story. Even *I* wondered how they would make me feel. I can tell you that thinking about the past still has the power to give me bad dreams. I still haven't seen the movie *What's Love Got to Do with It*. My feelings about Ike were raw and unresolved when the movie came out and I've never gone back. Would I have an easier time watching the musical?

The last time I'd contemplated my past I was in a clinic in Switzerland, sitting in a chair covered in antiseptic plastic and hooked up to a dialysis machine. I was uncertain about everything—my health, my future. But, at the opening in London, I watched my past unfold from the comfort of a plush velvet seat, the best in the house. I'm in a different place now, literally and figuratively—a different seat, and a different state of mind.

It's my story, but it's not me. When something bad is happening on the stage, it can't hurt me.

So I sat there and enjoyed it from afar. People expected me to cry. Instead, I was sitting there laughing. It wasn't funny, but it was strange, uncanny, you might say.

I practically did a double-take when Kobna Holdbrook-Smith came out onstage as Ike. It was as if Ike had come from the grave and stepped into that boy's body perfectly. Not only did he look just like Ike, he behaved just like him, too, with his exact speech and mannerisms. That's why I reacted so unexpectedly.

I have finally accepted my past, and I'm very happy that I can even laugh about it every now and then. I'm proud that my legacy is in such good hands. So much talent, energy, and heart is on that stage. Adrienne's transformation from a naïve country girl to a powerful woman is a sight to behold. And the end of the show is pure magic. "Tina" walks to the front of the stage, speaks directly to the audience, and announces that there's more to come. Then she leads a full rock band into an electrifying encore, just like I always closed my concerts. In a split second, Adrienne and Tina become one.

When the opening night audience heard the introductory chords to "Proud Mary," men, women, and *even* critics jumped to their feet and stayed there. I felt like I was back in the sanctified church. Everyone had the spirit, singing, clapping along, swaying to the beat. The applause continued when Adrienne led me to the stage to greet the people. I felt overwhelmed by their love and goodwill. And I had a special message for them.

Looking at Adrienne with admiration, I told the audience that now that I had found my replacement, I could truly retire. And I meant it.

Looking at Kobna Holdbrook-Smith, but seeing Ike, I told them, "I forgive him." And I meant that, too.

Before I spoke my final words, I thought about the evening, about the long road I traveled from Nutbush to this theater in London—all that I went through, from the beginning of little Anna Mae, all the way to here. And I thought, *I am blessed.*

Like the sweet and spunky child in the show, I had entered the world unloved, but I went on.

I lived through a hellish marriage that almost destroyed me, but I went on.

I faced disappointment and failure because of gender, age, color, and all the other obstacles fate placed in my path, but I went on.

I found happiness with Erwin, but as you now know, I almost lost everything . . . until love saved me. And still I go on.

———

My parting words to the audience that night—and my parting words to you—express the way I feel about the story of my life. Remembering the old Buddhist expression, I said, "It *is* possible to turn poison into medicine."

I can look back and understand why my karma was the way it was. Good came out of bad. Joy came out of pain. And I have never been so completely happy as I am today.

It took every bit of strength I had to get through my son Craig's memorial service. The worst thing any parent can experience is the loss of a child. (*Personal collection*)

CRAIG RAYMOND TURNER
1958–2018

"Hello, dear. I just want to hear your voice and that laugh of yours." I smiled when my son Craig said that to me because we always joked about how he called me "dear." Who calls their mother "dear"?

Our conversation didn't seem remarkable at the time—just the usual mother/son telephone catch-up. It was late June. Craig was in Los Angeles. I was home in Zurich. We were looking forward to his upcoming visit in August, when we planned to celebrate his sixtieth birthday. There were nights when we'd settle in for a really long conversation, sometimes watching an entire movie while we were on the phone (and making funny comments the whole time). But this wasn't one of them.

Craig told me that he'd met a woman who made him feel like he hadn't felt in years. "Mother, I'm really happy," he said. I was so pleased for him because I worried that he spent too much time alone. He also said that he was on his way to a chanting meeting, which was another positive thing. Chanting opens up the mind, the heart, and the spirit. In closing, he added, "You know you give me courage. You give me really good advice." Our affectionate words and casual banter seemed absolutely routine, making what happened just a few weeks later all the more shocking . . .

July 3, 2018, promised to be a really good day. Erwin and I were celebrating our fifth wedding anniversary and I felt strong enough to travel to Paris to attend my friend Giorgio Armani's fashion show. My recovery after my kidney transplant had been so difficult, so up and down, that I welcomed the chance to do something lighthearted. We had dinner with friends and spent the evening laughing and talking. By the time Erwin and I got back to the hotel, I was tired and ready for bed.

Erwin checked our messages and played one from our accountant regarding Craig that began with: "Turn off the speaker." He did, then disappeared into the next room to listen alone. And I thought, *Oh, what's Craig gotten himself into now?* I figured that he'd wrecked the car, or was in some bit of trouble like that.

But when Erwin came back, he was clearly shaken. He told me that Craig was dead. Not from an accident, the one thing a nervous mother always imagines. No, my son had committed suicide—he shot himself. I heard Erwin's words, but I didn't really understand their meaning. I froze. *This can't be true*, I prayed. I don't remember what happened next. What I thought or felt. There were tears and cries of disbelief. A stabbing pain in my heart. A night of raw emotion. And then questions, endless questions. Why, why, why?

I'll be honest with you. I'm certainly trying to be honest with myself. Craig was a troubled soul. I can still see him as a little boy, no more than two or three, wanting so badly to sit with me when I came home from a tour, but being told by Ike to go to his room. I'm sure in his little mind he didn't have any words to explain how much he wanted his mother, or his sense of loss, when I couldn't be with him. It wasn't my choice. It was the way we made our living. And of course, just when he got used to having me around, it was time for me to leave, and that meant being alone again. *Mother always gone.* It didn't matter if he stayed with my sister, my mother, or a trusted sitter. Craig didn't want them: he wanted me.

I think these memories stuck with Craig throughout his life. When he got older, and I was performing on my own, I tried to keep him close, even taking him on the road with me. But Craig had trouble fitting in because he wanted to be his own boss. I think that's when he began drinking. Eventually. he started attending AA meetings and he seemed to find them helpful. Unfortunately, his feelings of loneliness and insecurity always came back.

When Craig visited me in France, and later in Switzerland, he'd get quiet and sad when it was time for him to go back to Los Angeles. He'd say, "Here comes that feeling again," meaning loneliness. Whenever he brought it up, I tried to be supportive. I'd tell him "Okay, darling. If you feel that way you have to do something about it—find someone, live with them, marry them. You have to try to forget what happened in the past. Your life is changing now." I wanted him to remember how my life changed after I left Ike, how everything got better. He told me he was working on it and I believed him.

I thought he was making progress, especially after he said he was happy with his new job, his girlfriend, and his home, which he had just redecorated. Why, at this point in his life, did the darkness take over? Maybe he had gone back to drinking—apparently there were empty liquor bottles in the house when he died. Maybe that's what made him pull the trigger. I didn't even know he had a gun. I asked my younger son, Ronnie, where it came from. The terrible irony is that it belonged to Muh. She kept a gun, and when she died, Craig took it to his house and held on to it for all those years. I guess he thought he might want to use it one day.

I was shocked by the amount of planning that went into his suicide. The thought was there. Then the preparation. Then he did it. He wrote notes—he said that he loved me, he left instructions for his funeral, and he made bequests.

I arranged for a small, private service in Los Angeles for family and a few close friends. I didn't want anything public, with press and spectators. I wanted to remember Craig as he was, not focus on the way he died. The room was filled with beautiful pictures of him, with his easy smile, and gorgeous white flowers. Craig served in the navy after he graduated from high school. Because he was a veteran with an honorable discharge, he received full military honors at his funeral, including the presentation of the American flag and the playing of "Taps." I was so moved by these tributes and I kept thinking how proud he would have been to be honored that way. We ended the memorial by going out on a boat to spread his ashes at sea, just as we did for my mother and my sister. I threw a single rose into the water as my final goodbye.

I wanted just a few of Craig's things to remind me of him. His glasses—because I always teased him about the funny way he wore them on his nose. And the pictures he took whenever he came to visit me. I'm going to make a little shrine in my chanting room so he can be with me during my quiet times. I'm still trying to keep him close. He was fifty-nine when he died, but he'll always be my baby.

I know I'll get through this, somehow. I'm strong. I wish I could have passed on some of my strength to Craig, or that he could have found it in himself.

But what I really want is to hear my son call me "dear" again.

ACKNOWLEDGMENTS

There would be no love story, on the pages of this book, or in life, without my wonderful husband, Erwin Bach. April 7, the day he gave me his kidney and a second chance at life, is my new birthday. My gratitude and devotion to him are truly "river deep, mountain high." May we always make each other laugh, the true sign of a successful relationship.

I would sincerely like to thank my doctors. Without their knowledge and commitment I would not have survived my life-threatening disease. The foresight of Professor Doctor Vetter, the persistence and perseverance of Dr. Bleisch, and the confidence and professionalism of Professor Doctor Steiger, Professor Doctor Gürke, and Professor Doctor Heuss enabled me to be here today, writing these words. My doctors and the staffs at the University Hospital Zurich, the clinic at Zollikerberg, as well as the University Hospital of Basel saved my life, eased my recovery, and through it all, considerately respected—and protected—my privacy.

ACKNOWLEDGMENTS

I am grateful to my coauthors, Deborah Davis and Dominik Wichmann, for helping me to explore my past and tell my story. Our time together was as pleasant as it was productive.

And my thanks to Rhonda Graam, Roger Davies, Peter Lindbergh, Harry Langdon, Beat and Regula Curti, Sylvie Ackerman, Torsten Siefert, Andreas Bodenmann, Scott Waxman, and the Looping Group for their kind participation in this project.

INDEX

Tina Turner's legendary career has spanned more than fifty years. She has won numerous awards, including eight Grammys. After early hits such as "River Deep—Mountain High" and "Proud Mary," her 1984 solo album *Private Dancer* sold twenty million copies worldwide and included the hit singles "What's Love Got to Do with It," "Better Be Good to Me," "Private Dancer," and "Let's Stay Together." She played the Acid Queen in the 1975 film *Tommy*, and starred opposite Mel Gibson in *Mad Max: Beyond Thunderdome*. Her bestselling memoir, *I, Tina*, was turned into the Academy Award–nominated film *What's Love Got to Do with It*. One of the world's most popular entertainers, Tina has sold more concert tickets than any other solo music performer in history. She lives with her husband, Erwin Bach, in Zurich, Switzerland.

———

Deborah Davis is the author of eight books, including *Strapless: John Singer Sargent and the Fall of Madame X*; *Party of the Century: The Fabulous Story of Truman Capote and His Black and White Ball*; *Gilded: How Newport Became the Richest Resort in America*; *The Oprah Winfrey Show:*

Reflections on an American Legacy; *Guest of Honor: Booker T. Washington, Theodore Roosevelt, and the White House Dinner That Shocked a Nation*, which won the prestigious Phillis Wheatley Award for best work of history in 2013 and was nominated for an NAACP Image Award; *Fabritius and the Goldfinch*, which Amazon named one of the Best Books of 2014; and *The Trip: Andy Warhol's Plastic-Fantastic Cross-Country Adventure*.

———

Dominik Wichmann was editor in chief of two major German magazines for fifteen years: *Stern* and *Süddeutsche Zeitung Magazin*. He has won several journalism awards for his work as an editor and author. Recently, he wrote the book *Zwischen zwei Leben* for the former German foreign minister Guido Westerwelle. The book was a bestseller in Germany for more than sixty weeks and will be turned into a movie next year.

———

Remember when I said you'll never get out of this life alive? You won't. Whatever your expectation of what happens after death, or wherever you think you're going, you will not need your organs. But someone else does, and that person is anxiously awaiting a lifesaving organ transplant. Please go to **OrganDonor.gov** in the US or **BeaDonor.ca** in Canada to give someone the miraculous gift of life that Erwin gave to me.

Made in the USA
Monee, IL
27 May 2023

34712882R00163